Hafiz, Goethe and the Gingko
Inspirations for the New Divan 2015-2019

Hafiz, Goethe und der Gingko:
Anregungen für einen Neuen Divan 2015-2019

Published in 2019 by Gingko Library, *New Divan* is to be an
anthology of 24 poems, twelve by poets of the MENA region
and twelve from the West, inspired by the culture of the Other.

Building on the rich tradition of poets who have sought inspiration
from, and responded to, other cultures, and specifically to their poetry,
New Divan will demonstrate how the Other can be a source of
inspiration rather than fear. Each poem will appear in *New Divan*
in English and, where the poem was not written in English, both
in its original language of composition and in English translation.

Hafiz, Goethe and the Gingko
Inspirations for the New Divan 2015-2019

Hafiz, Goethe und der Gingko:
Anregungen für einen Neuen Divan 2015-2019

GINGKO
LIBRARY

First published in Great Britain in 2015 by

Gingko Library
70 Cadogan Place
London SW1X 9AH

What is the New Divan? copyright © Barbara Haus Schwepcke 2015
Arabic translation of *What is the New Divan?* © Nermeen Al Nafra 2015

Translation copyright *One Rosy Cheek* by Hafiz © Narguess Farzad 2015

The Droplet that Fathoms the Unfathomable © Mahmoud Dowlatabadi 1999
English translation of *The Droplet that Fathoms the Unfathomable* © Martin E. Weir 2015

English translation of *Song and Shape* by Johann Wolfgang von Goethe © Eric L Ormsby 2015
Persian translation of *Song and Shape* by Johann Wolfgang von Goethe © Rahim Gholami 2015

We on the Banks of the Euphrates © Joachim Sartorius 2015
English translation of *We on the Banks of the Euphrates* © Stephen Brown 2015
Persian translation of *We on the Banks of the Euphrates* © Rahim Gholami 2015

In the Manner of Abu Nawas by Joachim Sartorius © Carcanet 2006
English translation of *In the Manner of Abu Nawas* © Christopher Middleton 2006

The Desert by Adonis © Saqi Books 2015
English translation of *The Desert* © Abdullah al-Udhari 2015

Mulberry by Sabeer Haka © Sabeer Haka 2015
English translation of *Mulberry* © Nasrin Parvaz and Hubert Moore 2015

From Translation to Appropriation © Ahmad Karimi-Hakkak 2015

Goethe, Marianne and the Gingko © Insel Verlag Frankfurt am Main und Leipzig 1998
English text of *Goethe, Marianne and the Gingko* by Kenneth J. Northcott © 2003 by The University of Chicago

An Imagined East: Translating Goethe's West-Eastern Divan © Eric L Ormsby 2015

Interview with Daniel Barenboim by Wolfgang Behnken from *Funkelnde Hoffnung*
– A Spark of Hope by Georges Yammine, edited by Daniel Barenboim © Corso, Wiesbaden 2014
English translation © Darrell Wilkins
Arabic translation © Aran Byrne 2015

The rights of the contributors to be identified as the authors of this work has been asserted in
accordance with the Copyright, Design and Patent Act 1988.

ISBN 978 1 909942 82 0
eISBN 978 1 909942 83 7

Typeset in Optima and Adobe Arabic

A CIP catalogue record for this book is available from the British Library.

Printed and bound in Spain

www.gingkolibrary.com

Contents

Ginkgo biloba

Dieses Baums Blatt, der von Osten
Meinem Garten anvertraut,
Giebt geheimen Sinn zu kosten
Wie's den Wissenden erbaut.

Ist es ein lebendig Wesen,
Das sich in sich selbst getrennt,
Sind es zwey die sich erlesen,
Daß man sie als Eines kennt.

Solche Frage zu erwiedern
Fand ich wohl den rechten Sinn,
Fühlst du nicht an meinen Liedern
Daß ich Eins und doppelt bin.

d. 15. S. 1815

What is the New Divan?

Barbara Haus Schwepcke[1]

It all started with a poem, which Anthea Bell beautifully translated in memory of Werner Mark Linz when the pain felt at the loss of this inspirational man was still raw. For me, it perfectly symbolised his life, first as the founder of the New York publishing house Continuum and then as the Director of the American University in Cairo Press.

The gingko, that Eastern tree,
In my garden plot now grows.
In its leaf there seems to be
A secret that the wise man knows.

Is that leaf one and lonely?
In itself in two divided?
Is it two that have decided
To be seen as one leaf only?

To such questions I reply:
Do not my love songs say to you
– Should you ever wonder why
I sing, that I am one yet two?

Johann Wolfgang von Goethe sent this poem to his beloved friend Marianne von Willemer as a token of his affection. He pasted two dried,

1 **Barbara Haus Schwepcke** received her PhD in International History from the London School of Economics and Political Sciences. She is Chair of the Trustees of the Gingko Library.

crossed leaves from this ancient tree below the three stanzas and dated it 15 September 1815. The story of Goethe, Marianne and the gingko is brilliantly retold in this volume by the late great publisher Siegfried Unseld.[2] For the purpose of this introduction it is enough to know that Goethe, Germany's greatest poet and polymath, natural scientist, statesman and true cosmopolite, had picked the gingko leaf as a symbol of hope, long life and, above all, deep affection. The poem was his ode to friendship and symbolised the union between old and young, man and woman, human and the Divine, literature and scholarship, East and West – a union which in his mind was inseparable:

> *Know yourself and in that instant*
> *Know the Other and see therefore*
> *Orient and Occident*
> *Cannot be parted for ever more*

The poem became part of his *West-Eastern Divan*, which Goethe was inspired to write when he read the first German translation of the *divan* composed by the 14th century Persian poet Hafiz (Khwajeh Shams al-Din Muhammad Hafez). Goethe called Hafiz his 'twin' and decided to enter into a lyrical dialogue with 'the Other'. The Persian and Arabic word *divan* means 'assembly' and Goethe proceeded to assemble his own divan of 12 books of poetry, calling them *nameh*, the Persian word for 'epic poem'. He added a second part, 'Notes for a Better Understanding', which included a chapter on a 'Prospective Divan'. Considering his own Divan 'incomplete', it was his suggestion of how a divan might be attempted by poets and scholars of the future.

> 'At a certain period in Germany many imprints were distributed as manuscripts for friends. Whoever may find this off-putting should keep in mind that in the end every book is written only for an author's sympathizers, friends and admirers. I'd like to designate my own Divan in particular, the present edition of which can only be considered as incomplete. When I was younger, I would have had to hold it back longer; now, however, I find it more advantageous to assemble it myself than to bequeath such an undertaking to posterity, as Hafiz did. For the very fact that this little book stands there so, as I am now able to send it forth, arouses my desire to accord it, bit by bit, the full completion that it

2 Kenneth Northcott's English translation reproduced here with the permission of Chicago University Press and in the German original with the kind permission of Suhrkamp Verlag.

deserves. I now intend to indicate, book by book, and in proper order, what might still be hoped for from it.'

The *West-Eastern Divan*, published in 1819, was Goethe's very personal attempt to broaden the horizons of readers both ignorant and fearful of the Islamic world. From the time of the Persian Wars the Orient had been seen as alien, as a threat to the West – a threat, however, that was central to the formation of Western identity.

'To everything there is a season!' These words from the Book of Ecclesiastes open the scholarly essays that form part of the *West-Eastern Divan*. Today we face another era in which the West feels threatened by Islam, by the 'Other', by the unknown, which, whilst understanding very little about what this means, is all too often equated with religious fundamentalism. 'To everything there is a season!', Goethe said, and the season now seems right to attempt a divan for our times: a new divan.

The *New Divan* has a clear start and a grand finish: on the 15th September 2015 – exactly 200 years after Goethe sent his poem to Marianne – Joachim Sartorius, poet and former Secretary General of the Goethe Institut, will assemble a group of grandees, including the Syrian poet, essayist and translator Adonis, and the eminent author Mahmoud Dowlatabadi; they will select 12 poets from the East and 12 from the West, who will enter into lyrical dialogue with the Other. Their works will be translated either via bridging text or in a series of translation workshops, in which translators and scholars will work together with English language poets to create interpretations of the original poems. In other words, they will create new poetry inspired by the Other, and with it a further lyrical dialogue. All this will culminate in the *New Divan*, the assembly of '*Dichter und Denker*', poets, scholars and translators at the Barenboim-Said Akademie in Berlin in 2019, on the 200th anniversary of the publication of the *West-Eastern Divan*.

The volume you are reading is meant to be an inspiration for a new divan. Like the *West-Eastern Divan* and the gingko leaf, it is 'one yet two', part poetry inspired by the Other, part scholarly writing 'for a Better Understanding', on one side the original work and on the other the translation. It starts with a beautiful *ghazal* by Hafiz which has been translated by Narguess Farzad, and which, like most traditional Persian poems, does not have a name and is therefore known by its opening words 'One Rosy Cheek'. It is followed by 'Hafiz, The Droplet that Fathoms the Unfathomable', an essay that Iran's foremost novelist, Mahmoud

Dowlatabadi, wrote about the significance and influence of Hafiz's poetry and which he delivered at a celebratory gathering of *Dichter und Denker* in Frankfurt, Goethe's hometown, on the 250th anniversary of the German poet's birth. The English translation by Martin E. Weir and edited by Rahim Gholami is mirrored by the original text at the beginning of the other side of the book.

Joseph von Hammer-Purgstall's translation of Hafiz's *Divan* inspired Goethe to write his *West-Eastern Divan* and it is therefore right and proper to start this *Inspiration for a New Divan* not only with a poem by Hafiz but also one by Goethe. 'Song and Form' is followed by an essay, 'We on the Banks of the Euphrates' by Joachim Sartorius. He points to 'the playful integration of foreign literatures' as a defining feature of Goethe's late works: 'The most glorious evidence of this is undoubtedly Goethe's *West-Eastern Divan*. The poem 'Song and Form' stands in the opening section of the Divan: '*Moganni Nameh* – Book of the Singer'. The singer is unquestionably Goethe himself and the poems in his book take as one of their themes the poet's approach to the Oriental world, his enthusiasm for it and many links to it.'

Like the gingko leaf, Joachim Sartorius is 'one yet two': he is *Dichter und Denker*, poet and scholar at the same time. As the son of a diplomat he was exposed to the Other at an early age, which has inspired his writing ever since. His poem 'In the Manner of Abu Nawas' serves as an example of the lyrical dialogue, which the *New Divan* is meant to be. Abu Nawas was one of the greats of Arabic literature and inspired both classical Persian poets such as Omar Khayyam and Hafiz, as well as contemporary poets such as Joachim Sartorius and popular fiction writers like Andrew Killeen, who turns Abu Nawas into a detective.

'In the Manner of Abu Nawas'[3] is followed by Adonis's 'The Desert', which is from his bilingual edition of poetry *Victims of a Map*.[4] The Syrian Ali Ahmad Said, also known by his pen name Adonis, is one of the most influential contemporary poets of the Arab world. He was the first to complete an Arabic translation of Ovid's Metamorphoses and therefore represents the perfect continuation in the line of lyrical dialogues, which began with Hafiz and Goethe. His *divan al-shi'r al-'arabi*, an assembly of

---

3 Reproduced in this volume in both the German original (published by Kiepenheuer und Witsch) and in Christopher Middleton's English interpretation (with the kind permission of Carcanet).

4 'The Desert' (Diary of Beirut under Siege, 1982)' by Adonis, from *Victims of a Map: A Bilingual Anthology of Arabic Poetry* (Adonis, Mahmud Darwish, Samih al-Qasim), translated by Abdullah al-Udhari (London: Saqi Books, 2005). Reprinted here with kind permission from Saqi Books.

Arabic poetry spanning almost two millennia, has remained in print since its first publication in 1964. Thus, Adonis is one of the grandest of the grandees from the East to take part in the *New Divan*.

For the *New Divan* to succeed the poets need to be understood by the Other and for their work to be appreciated by the Other it therefore needs to be translated. The Indian poet Makarand Paranjape pointed to the inherent difficulty of this:

> *Yes, he wants to say, translating poetry won't be easy.*
> *How can it, if the poem itself is merely the translation*
> *of feelings so subtle that you barely experience,*
> *or so strong that you can hardly contain them?*

We have included in this volume a poem from the first volume, which Modern Poetry in Translation produced in 2015 and which had an Iranian focus, produced in collaboration with the British Council as part of their UK-Iran Season of Culture. In the case of Sabeer Haka's poems, the poet-translator Hubert Moore worked with Nasrin Parvaz, who produced a literal translation.

Since Hafiz's time poets have been a thorn in the side of the powerful. Narguess Farzad, whose beautiful translation of Hafiz begins the poetry part of this inspiration volume, describes the importance of poets for Iranians:

> 'They forever want to remind authority that power corrupts and it's been forever thus, from Shah Nameh's time to right now on the streets of Teheran there is this sense that you do not have a monopoly of control and power over the people. Of course they do it subtly, they do it very beautifully, it is many layed, it is a real filo pastry of layer upon layer until you get to the real core of the subject. One of my favourite contemporary poets, who died in the early 80s, he has this one line where he says the poets are inheritors of water, wisdom and light. The water is the passage of time, the tradition that we have, they have the added insight of wisdom and light. It is not darkness. They have to be enlightened. They are the prophets of our time.'[5]

---

5 From BBC Radio 4's *Through Persian Eyes* (http://www.bbc.co.uk/programmes/b01kjs1j)

Translation is also the theme of an essay in the scholarship part of this inspiration volume. Eric Ormsby, himself a poet and scholar, writes about what it is like to translate Goethe's 'Notes for a Better Understanding' for a contemporary readership. The centrepiece of the *Inspiration for a New Divan* is an interview with Daniel Barenboim, the founder of the West-Eastern Divan Orchestra. Here the maestro talks about the Barenboim-Said Akademie, where the *New Divan*, this dialogue of *Dichter und Denker*, will take place in 2019. In the hope that a dialogue based on mutual respect, talking with and listening to each other, will lead to a better understanding of the Other, the interview is reproduced here, with the kind permission of the Akademie, in three languages: German, English and Arabic. The latter leads into the part of the book which includes Mahmoud Dowlatabadi's essay on Hafiz in the original Farsi, Joachim Sartorius's comment on Goethe's *West-Eastern Divan* translated into Farsi and this introduction translated into Arabic.

A wood relief by Joseph Beuys, 1949

One Rosy Cheek

Hafiz[1]
Translated by Narguess Farzad[2]

One rosy cheek from the rose garden of the world is enough for us.
    In this meadow, the shade of that cypress, gliding by is enough for us.

Far be it from me, to keep the company of hypocrites
    Of the world's heavy burdens, a heavy cask is enough for us.

The Palace of Paradise is the promised reward for good deeds
    For us reprobates and rogues, the tavern of the Magi is enough for us.

Sit at the edge of the stream and watch life flow by
    This one glimpse of the transient world is enough for us.

Look at the cash in world's markets, and see the suffering too
    If this profit and loss is not enough for you, it is enough for us.

Friend is with us, what need to seek even more?
    Solace of the company of that soul-mate is enough for us.

Do not banish me from your door, not even to the gates of Heaven
    Of all time and place, the corner of your alley is enough for us.

Oh Hafiz, complaint against the springhead of Fate is unjust
    Flair like water and flowing lyrics are enough for us.

---

1 **Khwaja Shams-ud-Din Muhammad Hafez-e Shirazi** known by his pen name Hafiz (1325/26–1389/90). His collected works are regarded as a pinnacle of Persian literature and are to be found in the homes of most people in Iran who learn his poems by heart and use them as proverbs and sayings to this day. Adaptations, imitations and translations of Hafiz poems exist in all major languages.

2 Senior Fellow in Persian at the School of Oriental and African Studies in London, Narguess Farzard is an authority on classical and contemporary poetry.

گلـعذاری ز گلـستان جهان مـا را بـس   زیـن چمـن سـایه آن سـرو روان ما را بـس

مـن و هـم صـحبتی اهـل ریـا دورم بـاد   از گرانـان جهان رطـل گـران ما را بـس

قصـر فـردوس بـه پاداش عمـل مـی بخشند   مـا که رنـدیم و گدا دیر مغـان ما را بـس

بنشـین بـر لب جـوی و گـذر عمـر ببـین   کایـن اشـارت ز جهان گذران ما را بـس

نقـد بـازار جهـان بنگـر و آزار جهـان   گر شما را نه بـس این سود و زیان ما را بـس

یـار با ماست چه حاجت که زیادت طلبیم   دولت صحبت آن مـونس جان ما را بـس

از در خـویش خـدا را بـه بهشـتم مفرسـت   که سـر کوی تو از کون و مکان ما را بـس

حـافظ از مشـرب قسـمت گله نـا انصافیسـت

طبـع چـون آب و غزلهـای روان مـا را بـس

The Droplet that Fathoms the Unfathomable[1]

Mahmoud Dowlatabadi

Translated by Martin E. Weir and edited by Rahim Gholami

O Hafiz!
'To be as you are, what a delusion!'[2]

In pre-eternity, the rays of your beauty blazed in self-manifestation,
Love emerged and set the universe ablaze!
Your face manifested itself, but saw angels were bereft of love,
From jealousy, it was set afire, and engulfed humankind![3]

The worldview of Hafiz is as follows: Creation in love, from love and for love; and illumination as the coming into existence of the world with the very first manifestation. Since "Angels do not know what love is!"[4] humankind has become the locus of love, the eternal light kindled within humanity and man in the form of his Creator has received the "heft of the

---

1 Hafiz's *Divan* (ed. Qazwini and Ghani [future references are all to this edition], Ghazal 290, verse 3): "My heart entertains itself with the image of the magnitude of the sea, what a far-fetched phantom! / It is incredible to see what passes through the mind of this droplet when it fathoms the unfathomable!"

2 Goethe, *East-Western Divan*

3 Hafiz's *Divan* (Ghazal 184, verses 1–2); also the following are the remaining verses of this Ghazal: "Intellect sought to lit a lamp with that blaze, / The lightning of avid jealousy struck, and traversed the universe! / The pretender was adamant to be at the promenade of secrets, / The hand of the Unseen blocked the pass to the imposer! / Others drew lots, and they all turned to the high life, / Then it was our longing heart whose lot came as yearning! / The heavenly spirit fervidly longed for the dimple in your chin, / Hence, it cast a firm grip onto the ringlets of that curling lock! / Hafiz composed the mirthful book of your love on the very day, / When his pen drew a line over the chattels of the prosperous heart!"

4 Hafiz's *Divan* (Ghazal 266, verse 4): "O Cup-bearer, the angel does not know what love is, / send for a cup and spray rosewater on Adam's clay!"

trust"[5] with enthusiasm and wholeheartedly. The result was eternal and unquenchable longing; existence and being through an insurmountable quest for perfection and truth, surmounting a difficult trial to arrive at the source: to become "Him" with one's whole being.

In Hafiz's opinion, "intellect" (*'aql*) is an inadequate vehicle for understanding existence; since what set existence in motion is "love" (*'ishq*), and it is through love and 'illumination' (*ishraq*) that a person can take part in being and make it possible "to be".

With the *ghazals* of Hafiz as a criterion, Goethe recognises four principal themes in poetry: love, red-wine, the triumph of hope and aversion to odium – synthesised and harmonised in a manner that, as in the poetry of Hafiz, pleases the heart and elevates the spirit.

Such profound insight into Hafiz[6] through a second language is astonishing and praise-worthy. However, I doubt that an ordinary reader can manage to comprehend fully the poetry of Hafiz unless it is read in the original Farsi, and even then a progressive reading is necessary, a reading which persists through several years. For no human soul has the unending

---

5 Hafiz's *Divan* (Ghazal 184, verse 3): "The firmament could not bear the heft of that trust, / So, I was chosen, despite my madness, to carry out the task!"

6 It seems our age has witnessed a rediscovery of Khwaja Shams al-Din Muhammad Hafiz Shirazi (Hafiz). This has been a very sensitive and delicate process that owes its success to the scholarly achievements of minds as sophisticated as those of Mohammad Ali Foroughi, Dr Ghasem Ghani (my fellow townsman), Dr Fayyaz, the late Dr Parviz Natel-Khanlari, the late Abol-Qasem Anjavi-Shirazi, professors Motahari, Zarinkoob, and Meskoob, my precursors the poets Shamloo and Ebtehaj, and my colleagues Dariush Ashouri and especially Bahaeddin Khoramshahi who is one of the leading contemporary researchers of Hafiz and the Qur'an. The attention lavished upon Hafiz by such erudite and learned individuals, as well as many others among our compatriots, is yet more evidence of the poet's position with respect to Persian language, thought, temperament and conduct. Therefore we should be grateful to all the scholarly endeavours that grant us art appreciators the opportunity of becoming better acquainted with Hafiz from various angles. It was with this purpose in mind, and with a heart brimming with sincere and warm gratitude, that I too decided to explore the worldview, structure and nuances central to the poetry of Hafiz from my own perspective. Fortunately, the poetry of that "libertine (*rind*), i.e., Hafiz, whose lot in this life was longing for the beloved" (Ghazal 152, verse 5: "Others drew lots, and they all turned to the high life — then it was our longing heart whose lot came as yearning."), is so intricate and infinitely rich that it provides diverse perspectives for anyone who approaches the poet. I shall dedicate the short amount of space allotted to me here to commemorate Goethe for having introduced Hafiz to the West; and with a maximum of fifteen minutes per speaker, I once again found myself facing the problem of fitting an ocean into a jug. In the end, I wrote what the Creator (*ustad-i azal*) bade me to (Ghazal 380, verse 2: "From behind the mirror of the unseen [i.e., the heart], I am being addressed like a parrot, / Thus, I only speak that which the pre-eternal Master told me to say!"). In prose as concise as I can manage, I pray that I have gained some measure of success in this venture... and I offer my regards and respect to all scholars of Hafiz, to his admirers, to my countrymen, and to the memory of my father, "that diligent *rind*", who only ever spoke to us in the language of Hafiz, Sa'di and Firdawsi.

capacity to absorb and store so much meaning, aesthetic knowledge, infinite love and subtlety of wisdom. Therefore, it is best to read the *ghazals* of Hafiz in the same manner as they were written: gradually and over a period of more than half a century. A periodic reading of Hafiz never instils a sense of repetition in the reader — especially if his poetry is read in order to find answers to real life problems, that is, out of necessity — since in each creative reading a new concept may be encountered for indeed, "What passes through the mind of this droplet when it fathoms the unfathomable?"

Inevitably, Khwaja Hafiz, who could recite the Qur'an from memory in fourteen different styles of recitation and who regarded himself a droplet capable of contemplating the unfathomable mysteries of being, was born in Shiraz in 1325/26 and passed away in 1389/90. He died aged 74 or 75 and left behind nearly five hundred *ghazals* to be remembered by. His *ghazals* were compiled and published in a collection (*divan*) for the first time thirty-five years after his death. According to the sources, during the lifetime of Hafiz no one had the pluck to undertake this task.

In the time of Hafiz, book-washings and book-burnings were twice conducted in Shiraz during the reign of Mubariz al-Din Muhammad[7] on the pretext of eradicating philosophical books, and then again during the reign of his son and heir Shah Shuja, both of whom were vassals of the Ilkhanids and swore fealty towards what remained of the Abbasid caliphs in Egypt. Mubariz al-Din Muhammad, who was eventually blinded by his son, imposed so many restrictions upon people's lives with his prejudice and hypocrisy that he was given the title "*muhtasib*" ("market inspector"), and underground life became "the norm of the blighted libertines" (*rindan-i bala-kash*).[8] Mubariz al-Din Muhammad banned the teaching of philosophy in schools, dismissed muftis and sheikhs from Sufi monasteries (s. *khanqah*), prevented free-spirited scholars from assembling, turned the master of the Sufis into a major landowner and it is reported that even the city's grand Imam did not leave his cell except for Friday prayers, and he fasted and prayed standing and untiringly. The seat of judgement passed to the highest bidder[9] ... "The judge should not be addressed directly by any persons... and whoever confronts the judge, speaks daring words in his presence, disrespects him or displays insolence, we order the sheriff

---

7 Founder of the Mozaffarid dynasty. Shiraz was his capital, and he had a reputation for strict personal piety (*Encyclopedia Iranica*).

8 Hafiz's *Divan* (Ghazal 159, verse 5): "A person, spoiled with luxury, never finds the path to the beloved, / Loving is the demeanour of blighted libertines!"

9 *Shadd al-azar* by Mu'in al-Din Abu al-Qasim Junayd al-Shirazi

to chastise him!" … "Guile and hypocrisy, fraud and embezzlement, and cruelty and libel … making false oaths … deceit and debauchery among the populace, lack of shame, and bribery!"[10] were all dominant characteristics of the ruling class at the time. On the other hand, as well as suffering from the tyranny of their rulers, in order to avoid Mongol emissaries being billeted permanently in their homes, the people did not repair their houses. They buried their dead within the walls of their half-ruined homes, hoping that the emissaries would find this act abhorrent and not seek entry, since when they did enter they demanded food, fodder, wine and beautiful companions too!

Dominion[11] of the wise, prayer-house for the pure.

This was the title given to the city of Shiraz. And Mubariz al-Din Muhammad in imitation of the caliphs went on foot to Friday prayers.

* * * *

In my youth, I read the history of my homeland and I became so dejected and depressed that I constantly sought to drown myself in the joys and sorrows of literature, since from history there only emanated the odour of murder, the sound of ignorance clanging on ignorance, and the shedding of mankind's dignity through the annihilation of thought, beauty and freedom.

Yet, from what I can see in the *West-Eastern Divan*, the enlightened Goethe becomes enamoured with, and enraptured by, the splendour of content and form in the *ghazals* of Hafiz. This very vista opens his vision to the fantastical beauty of the Orient. And, it is through this perception that he recognises a necessity for intimacy between East and West, and toward the East there is no more edifying lense than that of Hafiz to provide a most fortunate motivation for this acquaintance. For, Hafiz is not only a successor to Sa'di, but his poetry is a refined portrayal of Dari-Persian. The language flourished in Rudaki, reached its epic heights in Firdawsi, and obtained its wealth of expression in Nizami, and then, having achieved a translucent pureness in the succinct works of mystics, was moulded into a new form by Rumi and polished by Sa'di. Now Hafiz was at the pinnacle of a language that in its core sustained an awareness of an ancient nation's trodden values in each *ghazal*, in each line and each

---

10 *Jami al-tawarikh* by Rashid al-Din Hamadani.

11 This is an allusion to the many diverse uses of the term *maqam* (lit. state, station, residence) in the *ghazals* of Hafiz.

word that the poet mounted as a diamond upon his "Ring of Solomon" (*angushtar-i Sulayman*).[12]

Hafiz received formal education, then "he gave away the lesson, learned during the early morning prayers, on the path to the tavern"[13] and adopted the "demeanour of the libertines". He knew Arabic and Arabic poetry, and was an accomplished musician and singer. Even so, his wisdom goes beyond the philosophy and literature of post-Islam. Indeed, in his *ghazals* artistic reflection finds expression in ancient and contemporary wisdom, sun worship, Manicheism, Zoroastrianism, myths and history and astronomy as well as Greek philosophy. Wine and the beloved, the cup-bearer and the beautiful youth, the minstrel and the lover, the magi and the libertine, the wise old man and the disciple are present in the company of sheikhs, ascetics, Sufis and sheriffs. However they all appear in the *ghazals* of Hafiz in roles that defy stereotypes. The sun, light, radiance, moonlight, aurora, dawn, sunrise and the rising star are all symbols of immortality and eternity in the poetry of Hafiz, and are constantly in opposition to the darkness[14], despondency, deceit, dishonesty and treachery of the times.

Nor must we forget that the poetry of Hafiz is fragrant! It embraces flowers and spring and the breeze, it is in the colour of moonlight and of purple wine, which are presented all together to a friend, a beloved or one who is worshipped:

> The pupil of my eye is your home
> Honour us with your presence, this house is yours.[15]

The *ghazals* of Hafiz often dwell upon fond memories, reminiscing about "*shahryaran*" ("kings") and the "*shahr-i*" ("city") of "*yaran*" ("friends") in the "world-revealing cup" of Khusraw that no longer exists.[16] But, in addition to nostalgia, in the *ghazals* of Hafiz, as within our tattered and lost collective conscience, one inevitably encounters a manifestation of the spiritual identity of a nation.

---

12 Again, this is an allusion to the uses of the terms *Sulayman* and *angushtar* or *nigin* in Hafiz poetry.

13 Hafiz's *Divan* (Ghazal 371, verse 1): "On the path to the tavern we gave away the lesson of the morning prayers, / On the path to the beloved we sacrificed the summit of all our prayers."

14 Hafiz's *Divan* (Ghazal 232, verse 3): "The company of tyrannical governors is the perpetual darkness of the winter solstice, / Seek light from the sun and await the sunrise!"

15 Hafiz's *Divan* (Ghazal 34, verse 1).

16 In Persian mythology, the Cup of Kay Khusraw was a divination instrument.

With regard to its formal structure, the poetry of Hafiz suggests the geographical, environmental essence and the characteristics that define ancient Iranian architecture! Similarly, and from a behaviourist point of view, Hafiz is the epitome of an Iranian intellectualism in absolute harmony with Iran's geography and clime. His poetry betrays a tendency towards humour and playfulness, acquired under oppression, to be realised in flexibility and adaptability, and from which the appelation *rind* ("one whose exterior is liable to censure, but who at heart is sound")[17]is derived. It is with this understanding that poetic tone, diction and even words in Hafiz can be perceived as crescent, arched, rippled and ephemeral: resembling rippled sand, or the curling fishes of being in the waves of existence, or the symmetry found in domes and passageways. And with regard to these roofs, octagonal vestibules, thresholds, passageways, niches, casements, mantels, private and public courts, the arches in the cradling domes, ceilings and terraces, turrets and closets, labyrinthine spaces that obviate amphiboly and mirror both covert and overt psychological and spiritual characteristics — why should these architectural features not find a vivid counterpart in the *ghazal*, in the rhythm and the pauses within each sentence?

> *The Rose at my side, the wine-cup in the palm of my hand,*
> *and the beloved in my embrace!*[18]

No doubt, the average Iranian reader, confronted by the poetry of Hafiz, does not feel compelled to ask, 'Where does this or that thought come from?' since he has in his collective consciousness a grasp of the visceral, national implications hidden in the poems. This explains why Iranian people are able to feel close to Hafiz who by means of incredible impartiality and considerateness was able to promote unity and peace in spite of historical and religious discord. At the same time, Hafiz himself remains dynamic while navigating between the most mundane daily concerns and the most sublime aspirations, with the hope of touching "that inverted turquoise dome"[19] and hearing the musical harmony of existence, in order to remain in a state of such constant evolution that it seems that the 'libertine' "whose lot in this life was longing for the beloved" has stepped above a brick-walled alley to ascend into the orbit of being, to arrive at the very beginning, when:

---

17 Steingass, s.v., after the *Burhan-i Qati'*.

18 Hafiz's *Divan* (Ghazal 46, verse 1): "The Rose at my side, the wine-cup in the palm of my hand, and the beloved in my embrace, / On a day such as this, the king of the world would wish to be my slave!"

19 The sky.

Love emerged and set the universe ablaze![20]

* * * *

At any rate, Hafiz was taken to the court for ethical inquisition as well, from envy no doubt, but under a pretext that his poetry is unorthodox. And, it was in such circumstances that housewives were obligated to wash and tear apart his poetry.

Belittling love, yes. Love was treated with disdain:

What a swindle that pottery supersedes jewellery in the market,
No doubt if blood flows from the jewel's heart![21]

I have often pondered whether there has been any concept conceivable by the mind of mankind that has not been examined by Hafiz. Is there any word that does not appear in the poetry of Hafiz unless in its best possible place and usage? Are there any questions about human nature, which Hafiz has not contemplated? It must not be assumed that an absence of evolution of the Persian language has been the reason for the appreciation of Hafiz by both academic and non-academic readers. Farsi has not remained unchanged and it should be noted that Hafiz is not as easy to read as it might seem. But, the secret behind the language of Hafiz is that it does not reject anyone who appeals to it. The poet's mystery is shared by all and every one of his readers, and whoever reads his poetry finds his or her lot therein. Hafiz is consulted for every predicament, be it a matter of love, sorrow, defeat, misery, madness, denial, fate, hopelessness, bondage or freedom. That is why among Iranians Hafiz is known as one who speaks the tongue of the unknown, one who does not leave you without an answer. Hafiz is a master of figurative speech, a fact to which he himself refers in many places. Therefore, to bestow this title upon Hafiz signifies the awareness of our collective receptivity to the mysteriousness of his language and diction. Those mysteries and secrets that in both structure and meaning manifest themselves in spans and spasms, in circular, evasive and multi-angled formations, essentially unifying and multiplying themselves in cosmic imitation, while all the while extruding hope from the depths of hopelessness.

In a similar vein, Hafiz is an example of the Iranian scholar's propensity to overcome difficulties with a flexibility and delicacy reminiscent of

20 See footnote 3.

21 Hafiz's *Divan* (Ghazal 277, verse 3).

miniature painting, with the ability to remain patient in suffering, to regard life through a transient lens in the manner of Omar Khayyamm, to pay attention to detail, to be adaptable and lenient, to cherish contentment, generosity and enterprise, and to maintain an indifference towards the world and worldly vanities.[22]

Seek light from the sun, and await the sunrise![23]

Moreover the most obvious reason for our general inclination towards Hafiz is the similarity of his times to those that succeeded his, and the circumstances that followed afterward that seem to have become so degraded and decadent that not a single water-lily bloomed in the mire of those later centuries. Darkness became ever more dominant. This is why Hafiz has been recognised as both the apex and conclusion of the Persian *ghazal* tradition. After Hafiz, desolation and degeneration formed such deep and expansive roots that it would be easy to assume that reading his poetry must not have been a simple task. As such, how is it possible for the Iranian sensibility — that of a people who in every time and age have been forced to retreat into themselves — to separate itself from Hafiz and his sympathetic poetry? How is it possible for us not to admire this eternal custodian of our consciousness and of the essence of truth, which he preserves in his conscience? Hafiz has been and still is the ultimate hope of any Iranian person in their most volatile and vulnerable moments. He has been and will be the boon companion and the purveyor of joy and hope in times of celebration. He is at all times at war with evil and wickedness and an admirer of beauty. His poetry is the language of love: from the most earthly and achievable love, to love in its capacity to divulge the very meaning of existence — and by the latter I mean love for the origin of humanity and the very essence of Creation.

* * * *

Of course, the genius of Hafiz, that "droplet that fathoms the unfathomable", is in his ghazals, their creative expression and their wealth of meaning. However, I tend to think that the miracle of Hafiz is also in his life and demeanour throughout his encounter with both the realms of love and

---

22 Hafiz's *Divan* (Ghazal 346, verse 10): "Although I am drenched in poverty, shame upon me, / If I succumb to dipping my frock in the pool of the sun [beg from others]!"

23 Hafiz's *Divan* (Ghazal 232, verse 3): "The company of tyrannical governors is the perpetual darkness of the winter solstice, / Seek light from the sun and await the sunrise!"

destruction. In other words, his standing and yet not falling — bending like a stalk of wheat and yet enduring and not breaking, until he was able to take to its destination his lot from "the heft of the trust"[24] — and, to be fair, he did the job most excellently, since:

> *None like Hafiz could strip the veil from face of thought,*
> *Since the locks of speech have been combed with quill pens!*[25]

Mahmoud Dowlatabadi[26]
9 August 1999, Tehran

---

24 See footnote 5.

25 Hafiz's *Divan* (Ghazal 184, verse 7).

26 **Mahmoud Dowlatabadi** is one of the Iran's most important writers. Born in 1940 in a remote farming region of Iran, the son of a shoemaker, he spent his early life and teens as an agricultural day labourer until he made his way to Tehran, where he began writing plays, stories and novels. Dowlatabadi pioneered the use of the everyday language of the Iranian people as suitable for high literary art. His books include *Missing Soluch*, his first work to be translated into English, and a ten-book portrait of Iranian village life, *Kelidar*. In 1974, Dowlatabadi was arrested by the Savak, the Shah's secret police. When he asked what crime he'd committed, he was told, 'None, but everyone we arrest seems to have copies of your novels, so that makes you provocative to revolutionaries.' He was in imprisoned for two years. His 2013 novel *The Colonel* was shortlisted for the Haus der Kulturen der Welt Berlin International Literature Award, longlisted for the Man Asian Literary Prize, and the winner of the 2013 Jan Michalski Prize for Literature. *Thirst*, published in 2014 in its English translation, is a powerful novel of the Iran-Iraq war.

Song and Shape by Johann Wolfgang von Goethe

Translated by Eric L Ormsby[1]

Let the Greek knead shapeless clay
into forms quite clarified,
let the son of his hands display
delight intensified.

But for us it is ecstatic
flowing Euphrates to grip,
to ramble, ripple-erratic,
into its spilling slip.

If then I drown soul`s blaze,
Song, you will yet ring clear.
When the poet`s pure hand plays
water itself forms a sphere.

---

1 **Eric Linn Ormsby**, born in Atlanta in 1941, is a poet, a scholar, and a man of letters. He was a longtime resident of Montreal, where he was the Director of University Libraries and subsequently a professor of Islamic thought at McGill University Institute of Islamic Studies. He was Professor and Senior Research Associate at the Institute of Ismaili Studies in London until his retirement in 2013.

Lied und Gebilde by Johann Wolfgang von Goethe[1]

Mag der Grieche seinen Thon
Zu Gestalten drücken,
An der eignen Hände Sohn
Steigern sein Entzücken;

Aber uns ist wonnereich
In den Euphrat greifen,
Und im flüßgen Element
Hin und wieder schweifen.

Löscht ich so der Seele Brand
Lied es wird erschallen;
Schöpft des Dichters reine Hand
Wasser wird sich ballen.

1 **Johann Wolfgang von Goethe** (1749-1832). Arguably Germany's greatest poet, Goethe was also novelist, playwright, natural philosopher, diplomat and civil servant. With Friedrich Schiller he was the main representative of the *Sturm und Drang* literary movement and the Weimar Classicism. His best-known works are *Faust, The Sorrows of Young Werther, Italian Journey* and *West-Eastern Divan*.

We on the banks of the Euphrates[1]

Joachim Sartorius[2]

Translated by Stephen Brown

The playful integration of foreign literatures is a defining feature of the light and floating artistry of late Goethe. This much is familiar: Goethe was a cosmopolitan in his bones, widely travelled and supremely accomplished in his dealings with the Other.

Yet, time and again, that playful aesthetic, which understands the alien as part of its own inclination, delights us in new ways. The most glorious evidence of this is undoubtedly Goethe's 'West-East Divan'. The poem 'Song and Shape' stands in the opening section of the 'Divan': '*Moganni Nameh* – Book of the Singer'. The singer is unquestionably Goethe himself and the poems in his book take as one of their themes the poet's approach to the Oriental world, his enthusiasm for it and many links to it.

To simplify greatly, we can say that the 'West-East Divan' owes its origin to two powerful stimuli: in 1814 Goethe's discovery of the Persian poet Hafiz in Josef von Hammer's translation, published in that year, and in the summer of 1815 his late-in-life passion for Marianne von Willemer, the young and vivacious wife of a banker.

---

1 Persian translation see pages: ٢–١٧

2 **Joachim Sartorius** was born 1946 in Fürth/Franconia and grew up in Tunis. He worked as a diplomat in New York, Istanbul, Prague and Nicosia. After holding various positions in the field of international cultural policy he became head of the Goethe Institute and then – from 2001 to 2011 – Director General of the Berlin Festivals. He has received fellowships from the Rockefeller Foundation and Collegium Budapest and was elected a member of the German Academy for Language and Literature in 2002. His wide-ranging publishing projects include translations of the Collected Works of Malcolm Lowry and William Carlos Williams, as well as works by John Ashbery and Wallace Stevens. His own poetry has been collected in seven volumes, most recntly *Hôtel des Étrangers* (2008). He was recently awarded the Paul Scheerbart Prize for his translations of contemporary American poetry.

We can see the traces of these two illuminating influences in 'Song and Shape': 'soul's blaze' is Goethe's love for the young woman, unfulfilled, disguised and soon to be abandoned, in deference to the Court in Weimar and to his wife Christiane von Goethe; the 'ripple-erratic' is the poetry of the Orient, a poetry without boundaries, fluent and open in form. The poem may arise from mental agonies, but it shapes those agonies, 'quenches' and so overcomes them.

The origins of the 'Divan' are rooted in Goethe's literary expedition into the 'pure Orient', into – as he once put it – 'Man's original homeland'. Though it was Hafiz who crystallised his reflections on poetics, Goethe engaged with the broad range of Middle Eastern culture. He read all the then published traveller's accounts of the Middle East, Persia and Central Asia. We know of his earnest efforts to learn the calligraphy of the region: he had 'Suleika' embroidered in Persian script in the slippers he gave to Marianne von Willemer.

Goethe knew that poetry – as he understood it then and as we still understand it today – had its beginnings on the banks of the Euphrates and the Tigris. The French writer Maurice Blanchot reports that the ancient Sumerians scratched symbols of their dreams onto lumps of clay and then threw them into the river. The lumps of clay, argues Blanchot, prefigure the book and the poem; the river, the public. Goethe identified himself with these ancient traditions. He refers explicitly to Mesopotamia, naming the Euphrates in his poem. By 'us' he means the poets of the Orient and that he includes himself in their ranks.

Against them he sets 'the Greek'. And yet, by choosing as his example of the plastic arts of antiquity not, as would be more usual, the sculpting of marble but rather the kneading and shaping of wet clay, Goethe ensures the contrast with the 'ripple-erratic' of the East is not so great that we might suspect him of an 'anti-classical' turn. Goethe, who after all formerly modelled himself on the Greeks, seeks rather to establish the affinity between the sculptors of classical Greece and the Persian poets of the Middle Ages, in accordance with the vision he proclaims throughout the 'Divan', a vision, that is, of a world in which Orient and Occident are inextricably linked.

The Greek's rapture in the work he has created is probably a reference to the story of Pygmalion in Ovid, who fell in love with the statue he himself had carved out of ivory, or to the myth of Prometheus, who shaped mud into men, into whom Athena then breathed life. He contrasts this 'rapture' with the bliss of the poets of the Orient who reach into the Euphrates and extinguish their turmoil in a song.

The last lines of the poem describe a miracle: the water rolls itself into a song, into a perfectly 'round' form in the 'poet's pure hand'. Hendrik Birus has pointed out a similar formulation in a text by Jacob Grimm. In his foreword to Hartman von Aue's 'Poor Heinrich' of 1815, Grimm writes that 'outside of folk literature, only the great poets of all ages are granted the gift of gathering water into a ball with their pure hands, water which others must pour into mundane vessels to carry.'

Everything in the poem is in movement, a beautiful to and fro, to the point of being, as it were, 'water itself forming a sphere'. But the true miracle is how a poem weighted with great themes exudes such a brilliant ease.

In the Manner of Abu Nuwus

Joachim Sartorius

Translated by Christopher Middleton[1]

> The summer stars up there discover
> a clearing. Down they shine
> on pots of wine we stop with wet
> turbans of clay that catch the glow.
>
> Wine wakes the heart for hunting. Hills
> and antilope it promises. Drink up, it says,
> enjoy, for nothing of remembered life
> is left but freshness of the single senses.
>
> A shelled almond's aroma.
> Your silver necklace, tinkling.
> A green and soft light
> in the gardens of Basra.
>
> Shall we drink up then to good old times?
> To the dune's ridge, whiter
> than white, whiter still than paper –
> do you recall these words of mine on it?
>
> And to the parrot, redder than red, perching
> beside a turban? Redder than blood?
> Do you recall the blood? Recall, chirping
> themselves to their long death in us, the cicadas?[2]

1 **John Christopher Middleton** served in the Royal Air Force and later studied at Merton College, Oxford, graduating in 1948. He has held academic positions at the University of Zürich and King's College London. In 1966 he took up a position as Professor of Germanic Languages & Literature at the University of Texas, Austin, retiring in 1998. Middleton has published translations of Robert Walser, Nietzsche, Hölderlin, Goethe, Gert Hofmann and many others. He has received various awards, including the Geoffrey Faber Memorial Prize and the Schlegel-Tieck Prize for translation.

2 This translation is reproduced with the kind permission of Carcanet Press.

In der Art des Abu Nawas[3]

Joachim Sartorius

Die Sommersterne finden ihre Lichtung
im Himmel. Sie leuchten auf die Weinkrüge
herab, ihren Turban aus feuchtem Lehm.

Der Wein weckt das Jagdherz. Er verspricht
Hügel und Wild. Trink, sagt er, koste, denn
vom erinnerten Leben bleibt nichts als die Frische

einzelner Sinne. Der Duft der aufgeschlagenen Mandel.
Das Klingeln der Silberkette an deinem Kinn.
Das Licht, grün und sanft, in den Gärten von Basra.

Trinken wir auf die vergangenen, die schönen Tage!
Auf den Dünenkamm, weißer als weiß, weißer als
die Seite? Erinnerst du meine Worte auf der Seite?

Und den Papagei, röter als rot, neben dem Turban?
Röter als Blut? Erinnerst du das Blut? Erinnerst du
die Zikaden, die sich in uns zu langem Tode zirpten?

---

3 **Abu Nuwas, al-Hasan** b. Hani b. al-Sabbah al-Hakami al-Farsi al-Ahwazi (b.139 or 140/756–8, d.
between mid-198 and early 200/813–5) was one of the most famous poets of the early 'Abbasid period.
He was born in the province of Ahwaz and died in Baghdad.

The Desert
(The Diary of Beirut Under Siege, 1982)

Adonis[1]
Translated by Abdullah al-Udhari

1

My era tells me bluntly:
You do not belong.
I answer bluntly:
I do not belong,
I try to understand you.
Now I am a shadow
Lost in the forest
Of a skull.

2

I'm on my feet, the wall is a fence–
　　The distance shrinks, a window recedes.
Daylight is a thread
Snipped by my lungs to stitch the evening.

---

1 **Adonis** (the pen-name of Ali Ahmad Said Esber) is widely considered among the greatest living Arab poets. Born in Syria in 1930, he was exiled to Beirut in 1956 and later became a Lebanese citizen. He became a central figure in the Arab world's new poetic movement. In 1956 he helped establish the literary magazine Shi'r, and in 1968 founded its successor, the equally prestigious and influential Mawakif. Both played a seminal role in the revival of the Arabic literary tradition. He is the author of *Arab Poetics, Sufism and Surrealism* and, with Mahmud Darwish and Samih al-Qasim, *Victims of a Map* all published by Saqi.

الصحراء

أدونيس

(مختارات من يوميات حصار بيروت ١٩٨٢)

-١-

... في زمانٍ

يُصارحني: لستَ مني

وأصارحهُ: لستُ منك، وأجهَدُ أن أفهمَه

وأنا الآن طيفٌ

يتشرَّد في غابةٍ

داخل الجُمْجمَه.

-٢-

واقفٌ، والجدارُ سياجٌ —

مدًى يتضاءلُ، نافذة تَتَناءَى

والنَّهار خيوط

تتقطَّع في رئتَيَّ وترفُو المساءَ.

3

All I said about my life and death
Recurs in the silence
Of the stone under my head ...

4

Am I full of contradictions? That is correct.
   Now I am a plant. Yesterday, when I was between fire
      and water
   I was a harvest.
   Now I am a rose and live coal,
   Now I am the sun and the shadow
   I am not a god.
Am I full of contradictions? That is correct ...

5

The moon always wears
A stone helmet
To fight its own shadows.

-٣-

صخرة تحت رأسي، —

كل ما قلتهُ عن حَياتي وعن موتِها

يتكَرَّرُ في صَمتِها ...

-٤-

أتناقَض؟ هذا صَحيح

فأنا الآن زرع وبالأمسِ كنتُ حصاداً

وأنا بين ماءٍ ونارٍ

وأنا الآن جَمرٌ وورْدٌ

وأنا الآن شمسٌ وظلٌّ

وأنا لستُ ربًّا —

أتناقض؟ هذا صحيحٌ ...

-٥-

دائماً يلبس القمرْ

ليقاتِل أشبَاحَهُ،

خُوذَةً من حجرْ.

6

The door of my house is closed.
  Darkness is a blanket:
    A pale moon comes with
    A handful of light
    My words fail
    To convey my gratitude.

7

The killing has changed the city's shape – This rock
        Is bone
        This smoke people breathing.

8

We no longer meet,
Rejection and exile keep us apart.
The promises are dead, space is dead,
Death alone has become our meeting point.

-٦-

مغلق باب بيتي
والظَّلامُ لحافٌ:
قمر شاحِب، حامِل في يديهْ
حفنة من ضِياء،
عجزت كلِماتي
أَنْ توجِّهَ شُكري إليهْ.

-٧-

غَيَّر القتْل شكْل المدينة، — هذا الحجرْ
من عظام،
وهذا الدخان زَفيرُ البشرْ.

-٨-

لم نعدْ نَتَلاقى
لم يعد بيننا غيرُ نبْذٍ ونفْي
والمواعيدُ ماتَتْ، ومات الفَضَاءْ،
وحدَه الموت صارَ اللقاءْ.

9

He shuts the door
Not to trap his joy
… But to free his grief.

10

A newscast
    About a woman in love
    Being killed,
    About a boy being kidnapped
    And a policeman growing into a wall.

11

Whatever comes it will be old
    So take with you anything other than this madness – get ready
        To stay a stranger …

-٩-

أغلق الباب، لا لِيُقيِّد أفراحَهُ،

... لِيحرِّر أحزانَهُ.

-١٠-

— إعلان

عَن عاشقةٍ

قُتِلتْ،

عن طفل مخطوف،

والشرطي جِدارٌ.

-١١-

كل شيء سيأتي قديم،

فاصْطَحبْ غير هذا الجنون — تَهيَّأْ

كي تَظَلَّ غريباً ...

12

They found people in sacks:
    One without a head
    One without a tongue or hands
    One squashed
    The rest without names.
Have you gone mad? Please,
    Do not write about these things.

13

You will see
    Say his name
    Say I painted his face
    Stretch your hand to him
    Or walk like any man
    Or smile
    Or say I was once sad
You will see
    There is no homeland …

-١٢-

— وجدوا أشخاصاً في أكيَاسٍ:

شخص لا رأسَ لَهُ

شخص دون يديْنِ ودون لِسانٍ

شخص مَفْروم

والباقون بلا أسماءْ.

— أَجُننتَ؟ رجاءً

لا تكتبْ عن هذي الأشياءْ.

-١٣-

سوف ترى

قل اسمهُ

أو قل رَسَمْتُ وجههُ

مُدَّ يديك نحوهُ

أو سِرْ كما يسير كل راجلٍ

أو ابتسمْ

أو قُلْ حزنت مرةً.

سَوفَ تَرَىَ

ليس هناك وطنٌ ...

14

There may come a time when you'll be
    Accepted to live deaf and dumb, and perhaps
They'll let you mumble: death,
        Life, resurrection–
    And peace be upon you.

15

He wears Jihad uniform, struts in a mantle of ideas.
A merchant – he does not sell cloths, he sells people.

16

They took him to a ditch and burnt him.
    He was not a murderer, he was a boy.
    He was not …
                        He was a voice
Vibrating, scaling the steps of space.
And now he's fluting in the air.

-١٤-

رِبما جاء وقت ستقبل فيهِ

أن تعيش أَصَمَّ وأبكَمَ، لكنْ

رِبما سمحوا أن تُتَمْتِمَ: موتٌ،

وحياة، وبعثٌ —

والسلام عليكم.

-١٥-

يتزيًّا بزَيِ الجهاد، ويَرفُلُ في بَزةٍ من فِكَر

تاجر — لايبيع الثِّيابَ، يبيع البَشَرْ.

-١٦-

أخذوه الى حُفْرةٍ، حرقوهُ

لم يكن قاتلا، كان طفلاً

لم يكنْ ...

كان صوتاً

يتموَّج، يرقى على درجات الفضاءْ،

وهو، الآن، شَبَّابَةٌ في الهواءْ.

17

Darkness.
The earth's trees have become tears on heaven's cheeks.
An eclipse in this place.
Death snapped the city's branch and the friends departed.

18

You do not die because you are created or because you have a body
    You die because you are the face of the future.

19

The flower that tempted the wind to carry its perfume

                                        Died yesterday.

20

The sun no longer rises
It covers its feet with straw
And slips away …

-١٧-

ظلماتٌ —

شجر الأرضِ دمعٌ على وَجَنَاتِ السماءْ

والمكان انْخِسَافٌ، —

كسرَ الموتُ غصنَ المدينةِ وارتحل الأصدقاءْ.

-١٨-

لا تموت لأنك مِن خَالِقٍ، أو لأنَّك هذا الجسدْ

أنت ميتٌ لأنَّك وجْهُ الأبدْ.

-١٩-

زهرة أغوتِ الرِّيح كي تنقُّل الرائحه،

ماتتِ البارحَهْ.

-٢٠-

لم تَعُد تشرق الشمسُ، — تَنْسَلُّ في خفيةٍ

وتُوَاري

قدميْها بقشٍّ ...

21

I expect death to come at night
    To cushion his lap with

                  A rose–
    I'm tired of the dust covering the forehead of dawn
    I'm tired of the breathing of people.

22

From the palm wine to the calmness of the desert … etc.
From the morning that smuggles its stomach
    And sleeps on the shoulders of the refugees … etc.
From the streets, army vehicles,
    Concentration of troops … etc.
From the shadows of men, women … etc.
From the bombs stuffed with the blood of Muslims
    and infidels … etc.
From the flesh of iron that bleeds
    and sweats pus … etc.
From the fields that long for the wheat, the green and the
    workers … etc.
From castles walling our bodies
    And bombarding us with darkness … etc.

أتوقَّع أن يأتي الموتُ، ليلاً، —

أن يوسِّد أحضانَهُ

وردةً —

تعبت من غبارٍ يُغطي جبينَ السَّحَرْ

تعبت من زفِير البشرْ.

من نبيذ النخيل إلى هدأةِ الصحارى ... إلى آخِرهْ

من صباح يُهَرِّبُ أحشاءَهُ

وينام على كتف التائهين ... إلخ، (*)

من شوارع، من شاحناتٍ

للجنود، الحُشُود ... إلخ،

من ظلالٍ رجالٍ نساءٍ ... إلخ،

من قنابلَ مَحْشوَّةٍ

بدماء الحنيفينَ والكافرينَ ... إلخ،

من حَديدٍ يَنزُّ صَديداً وينزف لحماً ... إلخ،

من حقولٍ تَحِنُّ إلى القمح

والعشب والعاملين ... إلخ،

من قلاعٍ تُسَوِّرُ أجسادنا

وتهيل علينا الظلامَ ... إلخ،

_____

* تقرأ بلفظها الكامل، كما هي واردة في السطر الأول.

From the myths of the dead which speak of
    life–express life … etc.
From the speech which is the slaughter, the slaughtered
    and the slaughterers … etc.
From the dark dark dark
I breath, feel my body–search for you and him,
    myself and others.

I hung my death
Between my face and these bleeding words … etc.

23

Trees bow to say goodbye
Flowers open, glow, lower their leaves to say goodbye,
Roads like pauses between breathing and the words say goodbye,
A body wears hope, falls in a wilderness to say goodbye,
The papers that love ink,
          The alphabet, the poets say goodbye,
And the poem says goodbye.

24

The killer
In the air

من خرافات موتى، تقول الحياة — تقود الحياةَ ... إلخ،

من كلام هو الذَّبح، والذَّبح، والذَّابحون ... إلخ،

من ظلام ظلام ظلام

أتنفس، ألمس جسميّ — أبحث عنِّي

وعنك، وعنه، وعن غيرنا.

وَأعلّق موتي

بين وحيي وهذا الكلام — النَّزيفِ ... إلخ.

-٢٣-

شجرٌ ينحني ليقولَ وداعاً

زهرٌ يتفتَّح، يَزْهو، يُنكِّس أوراقه ليقولَ وداعاً

طرق كالفواصلِ بين التنفسِ والكلماتِ تقول وداعاً

جسدٌ يلبس الرمل، يسقط في تيهِ ليقول وداعاً

ورقٌ يعشقُ الحبرَ

والأبجديةَ والشعراءَ يقول وداعاً

والقصيدة قالت وداعاً.

-٢٤-

قاتلٌ

في هواء المدينة

Swims in the city's wound–
　　　　The wound is the fall
　　　　That shakes with its name
　　　　With its bleeding name
Everything around us.
The houses leave their walls
And I am
Not I

25

In a page of a book
Bombs see themselves,
Prophetic sayings and ancient wisdom see themselves,
Niches see themselves.
The threads of carpet words
Go through memory's needle
Over the city's face.

26

A star was drowned in blood,
The blood a boy was talking about
And whispering to his friends:

يسبح في جرْحِها، —

جرحها سقطةٌ

زلزلت باسمها

بنزيفِ اسمِها

كل ما حولَنا

ألبيوتُ تغادر جدرانَها

وأنا لاأنا.

-٢٥-

صفحةٌ من كتابٍ

تتمرأى قنابلُ فيها

تتمرأى النُّبوات والحكُم الغابرَهْ

تتمرأى محاريبُ / سجادةٌ من حروفٍ

تتساقَطُ خيطاً فخيطاً

فوق وجه المدينةِ من إبَر الذاكره.

-٢٦-

غرقت نجمةٌ في الدِّماءْ —

ألدماءِ التي كان طفلٌ يحدّث عنها

ويوشوش أصحابَهُ:

٤٧

Only some holes know as stars
Remain in the sky.

27

The night is daylight born black
    On this path.
Sunlight and candlelight are the same
    In the heart's darkness.

28

It's wrong
To convince the sun not to say
What's been written by the fields but not told by the seasons.

لم يعد في السماءْ

غيرُ بعض الثقوب التي سُمِّيت أنجماً ...

-٢٧-

ألليلُ نهارٌ يولدُ ليلاً

في هذي الدَّرْبْ

ضوءُ الشَّمس وضوءُ الشمع سواءٌ

في ظلماتِ القلبْ.

-٢٨-

خطأٌ أقنع الشمس ألا تقولْ

ما الذي دونته الحقولُ ولم تَرْوه الفضولْ.

29

The night descends (these are the papers he gave to the ink–
      morning's ink that never came)
The night descends on the bed (the bed of the
      lover who never came)
The night descends/not a sound (clouds. Smoke)
The night descends (someone had in his hands rabbits? Ants?)
The night descends (the wall of the building shakes. All the
      curtains are transparent)
The night descends, listens (the stars as the night knows are
      dumb,
      and the last trees at the end of the
      wall remember nothing of what the air
      said to their branches)
The night descends (the wind whispers to the windows)
The night descends (the light penetrates. A neighbour lies
      in his nakedness)
The night descends (two people. A dress holding a dress–
      and the windows are transparent)
The night descends (this is a whim: the moon complains to his
      trousers
      about what the lovers have always complained of)
The night descends (he relaxes in a pitcher
      filled with wine. No friends
      just one man turning in his glass)

يَهبطُ الليلُ [هذا

ورق كان أعطاه للحِبرْ — [حبر الصباح الذي لم يجىء]

يهبط الليل فوق السريرِ — [السريرِ الذي هيَّأه عاشقٌ لم يجىء]

يهبط الليلُ / لا صوتَ [غيمٌ. دخانٌ]

يهبط الليل [شخص — في يديه أرانبُ؟ نملٌ؟]

يهبط الليلُ [سور البناية يهتز. كل الستائر شفَّافَةٌ]

يهبط الليل، يصغي: [نجوم كما يعرف الليل خرساءُ، والشجرات الأخيرةُ

في آخر السورِ لا تتذكر شيئاً

من كلام الهواءِ لأغْصَانِهَا]

يهبط الليل [بين النوافذِ والريح همسٌ]

يهبط الليلُ [ضوء تسربَ. جارٌ يتمدد في عُريهِ]

يهبط الليلُ [شخصان. ثوب يعانق ثوباً — والنوافذ شفافةٌ]

يهبط الليلُ [هذا مزاجٌ: قَمرُ الليل يشكو لسروالهِ

ما شكاه المحبُّون دوماً]

يهبط الليلُ [يرتاح في جَرةٍ

مُلئت خمرةً. لا ندامَى.

رجلٌ واحدٌ يتقلَّبُ في كأسِهِ]

The night descends (carries a few spiders, feels at ease with
        insects which are a pest only to houses/
        signs of light: an angel coming, missiles
        or an invitation? Our women neighbours have
        gone on pilgrimage/come back less slim
        and more coquettish)
The night descends (enters between the breasts of the days/
        our women neighbours are my days).
The night descends (that sofa/that pillow: this is an alleyway,
        this is a place).
The night descends (what shall we prepare? Wine? Soup and bread?
        The night hides from us his stomach's appetite).
The night descends (plays for a short while with his snails, with
        strange doves which came from an unknown land,
        and with the insects not mentioned in the
        chapters of the book about reproduction among
        different animal species)
The night descends (thunder–or is it the noise of angels coming
        on their horses?)
The night descends (mumbling
        turning in his glass …)

يهبط الليل [يحملُ بعضَ العناكب، يرتاحُ للحشراتِ التي لا تسيء لغير البيوتِ. إشارات ضوءٍ: ملاك أتى، أم قذائفُ، أم دعوةٌ؟ وجاراتُنا كلهن ذهبنَ إلى الحج / عُدْنَ أقلَّ ضموراً وأكثرَ غنجاً]

يهبط الليل [يدخلُ بين ثديِّ الأيامى / وجاراتنا أيامى]

يهبط الليلُ [تلكَ، الأريكةُ / تلك، الوسادةُ: هذي ممرٌّ، وهذي مقرٌّ]

يهبط الليل [ماذا نُعِدُّ؟ نبيذاً؟ أم ثريداً وخبزاً؟ يخبىء الليل عنا شَهَيَّةَ أحشائِه]

يهبط الليل [يلهو قليلاً

مع حلازينهِ؛ مع حمامٍ غريبٍ ونجهلُ من أين جاءَ، ومع حشراتٍ لم ترد في فصولِ الكتاب الذي خطه اللقاحُ عن الحيوانِ وأجناسه]

يهبط الليلُ [رعدٌ — أم ضجيجُ الملائك جاءَتْ بأفراسها؟]

يهبط الليل [يهذي

يتقلَّبُ في كأسهِ ...]

٥٣

30

When the sun opens her bedroom for the evening
The seagulls appear as a cloth
Covering the face of the sky.

31

He wrote in a poem (I don't know where the road begins–
    and how to surrender my forehead to its rays)
He wrote in a poem (how can I convince him my future is a desert
    and my blood its mirage of sand?)
He wrote in a poem (who will shake the hardness of words off me?)
He wrote in a poem (you don't belong
    if you don't kill a brother …)
He wrote in a poem (what's going to happen is not what they expect
    and contrary to what's been thought …)
He wrote in a poem (how can we understand this fugitive language
    caught between the truth and the poem?)
He wrote in a poem (can the refugee moon embrace its cradle?)
He wrote in a poem (there's confusion
    between the sun's face and the sky)
He wrote in a poem (… /let him die …

— حينما تفتح الشمس مخدَعها للمساءْ

تتراءى النَّوارس منسوجةً غطاءً

فوق وجه السماءْ.

كتب القصيدةَ (لست أعرفُ أين تبتدىء الطريقُ —

وكيف أُسلم جبهتي لشعاعها؟)

كّتب القصيدةَ (كيف أقنعه بأن غدي صحارَى

ودمي سرابُ رِمَالِهَا؟)

كّتب القصيدةَ (من يزحزحُ صخرة الكلماتِ عنِّي؟)

كتب القصيدةَ (لست مِنَّا

إن أنتَ لم تقتل أخاً ...)

كتب القصيدةَ (سوف يحدث غير ما يتوقَّعُونَ،

ومَا يخالف كل ظنٍ ...)

كّتب القصيدةَ (كيف نفهمُ هذه اللغة الطَّريده

بين الحقيقةِ والقصيده)

كّتب القصيدةَ (هل سيقدرُ ذلك القمر المشرد أن يعانقَ شمسَهُ؟)

كّتب القصيدةَ (بين وجه الشمس والأفقِ التباسٌ)

كّتب القصيدةَ (... / فَلْيَمُتْ ...

32

The cities break up
The earth is a train of dust
Only love
Knows how to marry this space.

33

He is dead. Should I mourn him?
What should I say? Should I say: your life was a word, your
  death its meaning?
Or should I say: the road to the light begins in the forest of
  darkness?

Confusion … They are …
  I hide myself in a cave and close the doors with prayers.

المدائنُ تنحلُّ،

والأرض قاطرةٌ من هَباءْ:

وحده، الحبُّ

يعرفُ أن يتزوجَ هذا الفضاءْ.

مات. أرثيهِ؟ لكن

ما أقولُ؟ أقول: « حياتكَ لفظٌ ومَوْتُكَ معنىً؟ »

أم أقولُ: « الطريق إلى الضوء تبدأ من غابة الظّلماتِ؟ »

لغطٌ ... إنَّهُمْ ... /

تخبَّأتُ في غارٍ وأغلقتُ بابهُ بصلاتي.

34

He left the caravan train,
   Ignored its flute and its temptations.
Withering alone
   Drawn by a withering rose
   To its scent.

35

You will remain my friend
Of what was or what's left
   In this rubble
Oh, light that wears the clouds, the Lord that never sleeps.[1]

(4 June 1982–1 January 1983)

---

1 The Desert (Diary of Beirut under Siege, 1982) by Adonis from Victims of a Map: A Bilingual Anthology of Arabic Poetry (Adonis, Mahmud Darwish, Samih al-Qasim), translated by Abdullah al-Udhari (London: Saqi Books, 2005). Reprinted here with kind permission from Saqi Books.

-٣٤-

ترَكَ القافلهْ

ومزاميرَها وهواها /

مفردٌ، ذابلٌ

جذبته إلى عِطرها

وردةٌ ذابِلهْ.

-٣٥-

ستظلُّ صديقي

بين ما كان، أو ما تبقَّى

بين هذا الحطامْ

أيهذا البريقُ الذي يَلْبَسُ الغيمَ، يا سّيداً لا ينامْ.

(٤ حزيران ١٩٨٢ — أول كانون الثاني ١٩٨٣)

Mulberry

Sabeer Haka[1]
Translated by Nasrin Parvaz[2] and Hubert Moore[3]

Have you ever seen

mulberries,

how their red juice

stains the earth where they fell?

Nothing is as painful as falling.

I've seen so many workers

fall from buildings

and become mulberries.[4]

---

1 **Sabeer Haka** was born in 1986 in Kermanshah, Iran. He is now a construction worker and lives in Teheran. Two of his collections of poetry have been published in Iran and in 2013 he won first prize in the Iranian Workers' Poetry Competition.

2 **Nasrin Parvaz** became active in the field of women's and human rights during the Islamic Revolution. As a result of this she was arrested in 1982 and not released until 1990. She has been a refugee in the UK since 1993 and writes fictional accounts of the lives of the people in Iran and their struggle to change their situation.

3 **Hubert Moore**'s eighth collection of poems was published in 2014 by Shoestring Press. It takes its title, *The Bright Gaze of the Disoriented*, from a poem by Wojciech Bonowicz, translated from Polish by Elzbieta Wojcik-Leese, which appeared in Modern Poetry in Translation's *Transitions*.

4 Reproduced with the kind permission of Modern Poetry in Translation whose Iranian focus in 'Scorched Glass' (No.1 2015) was produced in collaboration with the British Council.

شاه توت

سابیر هاکا

شاه توت

تا به حال

افتادن شاه توت را دیده ای!؟

که چگونه

سرخی اش را با خاک قسمت می کند،

[هیچ چیز مثل افتادن دردآور نیست]

من کارگر های زیادی را دیده ام

از ساختمان که می افتادند

شاه توت می شدند!

From Translation to Appropriation[1]

Professor Ahmad Karimi-Hakkak[2]

Abridged by Rahim Gholami

A s readers separated from the literary culture of early twentieth
century Iran by the gulf in perception presented and upheld by the
discourse of *she'r-e* now, we tend to underestimate the part that various
literary borrowings current at the time played in the process of poetic
change. That is in large measure because traditional literary criticism
has led us to believe that poets like Bahar, Iraj, and Parvin are situated
within an existing literary tradition rather than positioned against it. We
still imagine these poets as writing in essential accord with inherited
norms and conventions, and fail to see clearly all the ways in which
they manipulated that tradition in order to make it relevant to their own
concerns. Traditional literary criticism in Iran tends to highlight visible
breaks with the tradition of classical Persian poetry as the distinguishing
feature of new poetry from the old, and this has dulled our perception of
those texts in which innovation may have taken other forms. All this has in
turn distorted our view of the processes by which poetic innovation was
conceived and implemented by pre-Nimaic Iranian poets. Many readers
have therefore come to associate openness to experimentation with
Nima and his followers. Because a poem can still be seen to be a *qasida*,

1 This is an abridged version of an article previously written as chapter four to the book entitled *Recasting Persian Poetry: Scenarios of Poetic Modernity in Iran* by Prof. Karimi-Hakkak. The original article provides a textual analysis of three poems by three distinguished Iranian poets after the World War I: 1) Improvisation: Bahar's *Toil and Treasure*; 2) Indigenization: Iraj's *A Mother's Heart*; and 3) Appropriation: Parvin's *God's Weaver*. However, because of the limitations of this volume, the present abridged version only covers the textual analysis provided for the first poem, i.e., Bahar's *Toil and Treasure*.

2 **Ahmad Karimi Hakkak** was Professor of Near Eastern Languages and Civilizations at the University of Washington and founding director of the Roshan Center for Persian Studies in the School of Languages, Literatures and Cultures at the University of Maryland. Karimi Hakkak has written nineteen books and over one hundred major scholarly articles as well contributing many reference works including the *Encyclopaedia Britannica*, *Encyclopaedia Iranica* and *The Encyclodedia of Translation Studies*.

a *ghazal*, a *qet'eh* or a *masnavi*, it is judged no different in its internal operations from the canon of such genres in the classical tradition. In other words, formal and generic conformity with the tradition has been taken as the sign of total adherence to the classical system of signification and communication. Conversely, difference in formal features has been raised to the status of the supreme sign of modernness.

As a result of all this, poetic innovations that preceded Nima have remained largely unexplored, buried under appearances of continuity and impressions of sameness. It is true that in Nima's later compositions, his innovative use of rhyme and meter make the difference between the modern and the traditional discernible. In those poems, in other words, departures from the traditional practice of poetry move to the apparent surface of the text. However, Iranian poets before Nima made significant contributions to a new construct of poetic themes, a distinctly "modern" mode of esthetic signification, and even a new and more flexible attitude toward rhyme and meter which find their final expression in Nima's later compositions. For example, the matrix of characteristics and relationships which we associate with the modernist trend in Persian poetry emerged and evolved in the increasingly open literary culture of the 1920s and 1930s. Consequently, we must turn to the generation of poets that preceded Nima in search of the beginnings of a process that culminated in his work. In this chapter, I intend to illustrate a central preoccupation of that generation, namely the way poets like Bahar, Iraj, and Parvin enriched and expanded the system of Persian poetry through their literary borrowings.

A Theory of Literary Borrowing

It is not so much that literary borrowings have gone unnoticed in the traditional articulations of the process of poetic modernization in Iran. In fact, the influence of translation from European languages is often acknowledged as a matter of course. Translation has been recognized as having played an important part in the process of literary change in Iran since the latter part of the nineteenth century, and that part has been seen to have grown in importance with the passage of time. Historians of Persian literature in the twentieth century have acknowledged the significance of translation as a component of modernity. It has become a cliché of the current narrative of literary modernization that translation from European languages resulted in the "progress" and "advancement" of Persian literature. In this, as in so much else, Rypka has served as a model for Iranian critics, and can be called upon to illustrate their views.

He observes that, in Iran, translation transformed the literary language in the latter half of the nineteenth century because "all the antiquated conventions, melismas and pomposities had to be done away with and an attempt made to accommodate the language to the demands of the original texts." And again, that "without these translations Persian belles-letters and the prose of the twentieth century as a whole is difficult to imagine."[3]

Arianpur adds his admiring astonishment to this assessment, speaking of a "strange passion and enthusiasm" (*shur o showq-e 'ajib*) for literary translation that took over the literary intellectuals of the nineteenth century. On the part that translation played in the emergence and evolution of literature in the twentieth century, he stipulates that translators had to follow "the manner of composition" (*shiveh-ye negaresh*) of their original texts, and write in simple and natural prose insofar as they were able to, shunning the use of "rhyming and artificial phraseology" (*ebarat-e mosajja' va mosanna'*). This, he asserts, resulted in greater simplification of Persian poetry and prose. "If it had not been for these translations," he concludes, "today's literary composition, which has approached the common parlance even as it has benefitted from the beauty of European literary prose, would never have come into existence."[4]

However, neither Rypka nor Arianpur, nor any other critic or historian, known to me, has made any attempt to show the impact of translation in specific ways. I am not aware of any attempt to come to terms with the bewildering variety of literary activities in twentieth-century Iran aimed at naturalizing literary texts of other cultures. Nor has any textual analysis been undertaken to illustrate the impact of such borrowings beyond general observations on personal choices and the dictates of the process of translation itself. Certainly, no critic known to me has examined the impact of translations on Persian poetry, its codes, or its traditional expressive strategies.[5] Moreover, critics seem to have taken the concept

---

3 Rypka, *History of Iranian Literature*, 342.

4 Arianpur, *Az Saba ta Nima* (From Saba to Nima), 1: 260.

5 In his and Cuypers's *Aux Sources de fa Nouvelle Persane*, French scholar Christophe Balay does make reference to the possibility of treating the choice of the kinds of texts to be translated as signifying some cultural lack, a collective intellectual desire of sorts, particularly in relation to the forms in which the native tradition sees itself as deficient. He refers to early Persian translations of European, particularly French, fiction as revealing the depths of the tastes and desires of the literary culture throughout the latter half of the nineteenth century. However, translation as an instrument of systemic redefinition and realignment still remains unrecognized, as there have been no attempts to demonstrate its impact at the level of the literary text.

of translation in the narrowest and most literal sense of the word, leaving out a tremendous variety of translation based textual activities. Naturally, implications of such activities for poetic change in twentieth-century Iran have gone unnoticed.

The reasons for this shortcoming are not far to seek. Acts of modeling based on foreign texts tend to complicate the categories through which traditional literary history attempts to articulate change. For one thing, processes of transformation involved in cross-cultural reproduction cannot be conveniently demonstrated through the methodologies of descriptive historiography. For another, the nature of the textual activity involved in such modeling activities often requires detailed analyses of individual texts, therefore precluding sweeping generalizations. Also, critics working in certain specific cultural milieus tend to underestimate the impact of all translation-based literary activities. Where original creative efforts are contrasted with literary borrowing, often viewed as a reflection of a cultural lack, tracing texts to their foreign origin may appear a little like an act of espionage. There may be other complicating factors which need not detain us here. Whatever the reasons, the part that literary borrowing has played in the process of poetic change in twentieth-century Iran has remained unexplored.

In a real sense, to say that in certain cultural circumstances literary translation plays a part in the process of esthetic change is to state the obvious. As Rypka and Arianpur have stated, since the late nineteenth century, translation from European languages, particularly French, has been a central preoccupation of Iranian literary intellectuals.[6] In order to assess the impact of more creative kinds of literary borrowing—adaptation, indigenization, or improvisation—we need to begin at the level of the text, and that would be possible, I believe, only if our analytical tools allow us to see the changes that texts undergo in the process of translation. As poets work to naturalize a foreign text, the specific textual manifestations of difference between what is poetic in the foreign text as compared with their general impression of the same concept in their native tradition becomes clear to them. This awareness, I contend, is fraught with possibilities for esthetic change. As critics, we can only attempt to reconstruct the process with reference to the texts involved. To do that, I need to introduce a few theoretical concepts that

---

6 Borrowings from other literary traditions in forms other than translation play a significant part in modeling activities of a systemic kind and consequently in instituting change in the native system. For a study of some ways in which the Persian literature of the modern era has borrowed from European sources, see Mohandessi, "Hedayat and Rilke"; and Beard, *Hedayat's Blind Owl*.

will enable me first to carry on with my textual analyses and then to integrate the potential of the process into an understanding of literature as a dynamic system. I suppose that when chroniclers of modernity in Persian poetry make reference to the impact of literary translation, they conceptualize the activity as a source of enrichment for the native literary tradition and as a facilitator of subsequent text-producing activities. In that sense, translation can be discussed as an agent of systemic change, accelerating and facilitating it by making available to writers and readers alike models hitherto nonexistent in the native tradition. The tacit assumption here is that in the exercise of judgment on text selection, on the specific activity of turning unintelligible sounds and symbols into signs and texts intelligible to native readers, and on the framing of the texts (including various acts of footnoting, captioning, or otherwise marking or identifying translated texts and the textual operations they contain) more is involved than free individual choices.[7] Indeed that judgment itself, I believe, is culturally determined and may be correlated with such things as assumptions about the original text's context, speculations concerning the need for the translated text, and expectations of the text's impact on the native literary or cultural system.[8]

* * * *

The system into which a translated text enters responds to it primarily in ways that relate to the system's view of itself rather than to the text's historical position or current status in the original system. If it perceives itself as relatively complete and in no need to change, it may undermine or even discard the text's differences as irrelevant or as signs of inferiority and assign the new entrant a marginal status. In this case the text's affinities with similarly classified texts tend to be accentuated. If, however, the system views itself as deficient and in need of change, it may give the text a central position, and thus allow it to play a significant part in the

---

7 Some of the best-known works of the twentieth-century Persian literature of Iran are marked as "based on" (*bar asas-e*), "modeled after" (*eqtebas az*), or "inspired by" (*ba elham az*) foreign, usually European, texts. Iraj Mirza's *Zohreh va Manuchehr* (Zohreh and Manuchehr), Parviz Natel-Khanlari's '*Oqab* (The Eagle), and many of Bahar's *qet'ehs* (fragments), are only some of the best-known examples. Specific studies of the ways such texts relate to the works that have given rise to them is an urgent task of literary scholarship in this field.

8 At mid-century, the compiler of an anthology of European literary works translated into Persian wrote in his preface: "There are many poets and writers whose works in their own languages are considered masterpieces of eloquence... However, as soon as such eloquent pieces are translated into another language, they leave behind all — or at least much — of their beauty and grace. A corpse is carried over to the other language, leaving its soul at home, very much like some sensitive flowers which, removed from their native clime, wilt away quickly and die." See Hamidi-Shirazi, comp., *Darya-ye Gowhar* (Ocean of Pearls), 2: ten.

process of change. What are foremost here, perhaps interpreted as signs of the foreign system's superiority, are the differences between this text and similarly designated native ones.

A corollary question arises at this point: can the body of translated texts existing in any literary culture at any given time constitute a system in its own right?[9] Clearly, as extrasystemic entities imported into the literary system of a given culture, translated texts correlate with that system in at least two ways. First, the principles of text selection are never quite random; they are often correlated with the native system's view of itself. Second, in the act of translation, the specific choices made and norms adopted are in themselves indicative of specific impressions of the native system. As a result, whether the corpus of translated texts can be viewed as a system, the assumption can be made that at certain junctures in the history of a literary system the corpus of translated literature amounts to more than the sum of its parts, that the body of literature translated from foreign languages comes close to constituting an internally structured entity with its own coherence, and that it interacts in some more or less meaningful way with the native literary system.[10]

* * * *

Theoretically, then, translated literature may affect a living literary tradition in diverse ways, now exposing its deficiency, now confirming its completeness. It may speed up or inhibit change, play an innovatory or a conservatory part. When it does contribute to systemic change, it may do so by expanding the literary system at the level of generic classification, thematic preoccupation, or expressive devices. It may offer new relationships between literary structures and social ones or among alternative thematic alignments; it may expand the thematic range or the expressive mechanisms of the native tradition. In all these cases, it makes a variety of new textual activities possible by providing examples which may have little or no precedence in the system. In sum, translated literature eventually contributes to change in the native tradition by displacing its center of gravity, disrupting the existing center-periphery formations, and changing the system's view of itself.

The implications of these theoretical assumptions for the process of poetic

---

9 At least one theorist argues that translated literature always constitutes "a body of texts that is structured and functions as a system." See Even-Zohar, *Papers in Historical Poetics*, particularly the section entitled "The Position of Translated Literature within the Literary Polysystem," 21.

10 Ibid., 22.

change ought to be obvious. The poetic system of Iranian culture at the beginning of the twentieth century was widely perceived as deficient in certain aspects and therefore in need of change. The introduction of alternative textual models through prose and verse translation was often undertaken with the purpose of remedying the perceived deficiency, and the texts thus generated were viewed widely as models to emulate. Selected from among texts considered central in the culture where they originated, such texts were manifestly different from certain central formations of Persian literature as stereotyped in the literary culture of the time. These works did in fact, as we shall see, give rise to a variety of textual activities based on nonnative sources.

* * * *

In this chapter we examine the manner in which certain European literary texts were incorporated into the poetic system of Iranian culture early in the twentieth century. As elsewhere in this book, I examine a limited number of texts and certain specific aspects of the activity. The poems I examine have all been conceived directly or indirectly as a result of their authors' contact with certain texts of foreign origin, yet they are remembered today not as translations but primarily as original compositions in the Persian language. Examining such works, on the one hand, in relation to the texts which may have given rise to them and, on the other, in relation to their generative ambience may well reveal the contexts and conditions in which literary traditions begin assimilating elements from other traditions; it may also shed some light on the ways in which literary cultures respond to such assimilations. A better understanding of both tendencies may then elucidate the process of change in an esthetic tradition.

Post-World War I Iran witnessed a bewildering variety of literary borrowings from Western literary traditions.[11] There were formal and generic imitations, blank-verse renditions, and a good deal of prose and verse translations of European poetic works. Regardless of generic type and formal features of the original texts, their Persian renditions were often made to accord more or less with the formal and generic classifications present in the Persian literature of the time. The kind of borrowing I examine in this chapter was no different. It was conceived as a sort of poetic improvisation on a topic thematized by some foreign text.

---

11 Iranian newspapers of the early twentieth century usually devoted a separate section to verse or prose pieces translated or based on European texts, often under the heading *Adabiyyat* (Literature) or *Adabiyyat-e Jadid* (New Literature). In most cases, these consisted of passages from larger texts such as novels or plays.

Most commonly, the poet would take the narrative and moral purpose of the original text and compose a Persian poem on it, the product often taking the shape of a Persian *qet'eh* (fragment) or *masnavi* (rhyming couplets).[12] The best-known example of this kind of borrowing remains Iraj's unfinished verse romance, entitled *Zohreh va Manuchehr* (Zohreh and Manuchehr), which is a masnavi in form. In all likelihood, this poem is indirectly based on Shakespeare's *Venus and Adonis*, or some prose version of the Greek myth in French.[13] The literary journal Daneshkadeh features scores of similar poems based on works by Boileau, La Fontaine, Rousseau, Platon, Goethe, Schiller, and others.[14]

Improvisation: Bahar's Toil and Reasure

Mohammad-Taqi Bahar's poem, *"Ranj o Ganj,"* (Toil and Treasure), is known to a great number of Iranians because it has been published in many generations of elementary textbooks in the last fifty years or so. It first appeared in January 1919 in the ninth issue of *Daneshkadeh*, and provides an illuminating example of the sort of borrowing whose nature and significance need to be examined. Here is the poem's text as well as my literal translation of it:

> *Boro kar mikon magu chist kar*
> *keh sarmayeh-ye javdani-st kar*
> *negar ta keh dehqan-e dana cheh goft*
> *beh farzandegan chun hami khast khoft*
> *keh miras-e khod ra bedarid dust*
> *keh ganji ze pishinian andar ust*
> *man an ra nadanestam andar koja-st*
> *pajuhidan o yaftan ba shoma-st*
> *cho shod mehregan keshtgah bar kanid*
> *hameh ja-ye an zir o bala konid*
> *namanid nakandeh ja'i ze bagh*
> *begirid az an ganj har ja soragh*

---

12 Perhaps this was because these "minor" verse forms were not identified with specific thematic concerns as much as were forms like the *ghazal* or the *qasida*.

13 Both Mahjub and Arianpur mention Shakespeare's *Venus and Adonis* as the sole source for the Persian poem. Yet, they both recount the differences between the two texts. Compare Iraj Mirza (Divan), 1963 ed., 244–53; and Arianpur (From Saba to Nima), 2: 401–13. It is entirely possible; I think, that Iraj may have been working from a French version of the Greek myth or a French translation of Shakespeare's play.

14 Of these, La Fontaine's fables have been reproduced in verse translations far more than all the others. In 1913 Ashraf al-Din Gilani, known as Nasim-e Shomal, published a complete volume of verse fables based on the works of La Fontaine and Florian. See Namini, *Javdaneh Seyyed Ashraf al-Din Gilani (Nasim-e Shomal)* (Immortal Seyyed Ashraf al-Din Gilani), 794–840.

pedar mord o puran beh ommid-e ganj
beh kavidan-e dasht bordand ranj
beh gav-ahan o bil kandand zud
ham inja ham anja va har ja keh bud
qaza ra dar an sal az an khub shokhm
ze har tokhm bar khast haftad tokhm
nashod ganj payda vali ranjeshan
chonan chon pedar goft shod ganjeshan.[15]

(Go work, say not: "What is work!"
for work is an eternal capital.
Watch what the knowing farmer said
to his sons at the time of his rest.
Said he: "Love your heritage well,
for in it is a treasure, hid by our ancestors.
I never knew where it was buried.
To search and to find it is up to you.
Come autumn, plow the entire field,
turn it upside down everywhere,
and in the orchard too leave no spot untilled,
seek out that treasure wherever it may be."
The father died, and the sons, hoping for treasure,
toiled much in turning up the field;
losing no time, with the plow and shovel, they dug
here, and there, and whichever way they could
As fate would, that year, for that good tillage
from each seed sprang seventy seeds.
No treasure was found, yet their toil
did turn out indeed to be their treasure.)

The poem is based on La Fontaine's "*Le Laboureur et ses Enfants*," the ninth fable in Book Five of *Les Fables*, and was printed together with a Persian prose translation of it with appropriate attribution. Here is La Fontaine's verse fable:

Travaillez, prenez de la peine:
C'est le fonds qui manque le moins.
Un riche Laboureur sentant sa mort prochaine

---

15 This poem was first published in *Daneshkadeh*, no. 9 (January 21, 1919): 505–6. It has been reprinted in successive editions of Bahar's *Divan* with no reference to the poem's origin. For the latest edition, see Bahar, *Divan-e Ash'ar-e Shadravan Mohammad-Taqi Bahar Malek al-Sho'ara* (Poetic Divan). For the text of the poems, see vol. 2: 1108.

Fit venir ses enfants, leur parla sans témoins.
Gardez-vous, leur dit-il, de vendre l'héritage
Que nous ont laissé nos parents.
Un trésor est caché dedans.
Je ne sais pas l'endroit; mais un peu de courage
Vous le fera trouver, vous en viendrez à bout.
Remuez votre champ dès qu'on aura fait l'août.
Creusez, fouillez, bêchez, ne laissez nulle place
Où la main ne passe et repasse.
Le Père mort, les fils vous retournent le champ
Deçà, delà, partour; si bien qu'au bout del'an
Il en rapporta davantage.
D'argent, point de caché. Mais le Père fut sage
De leur montrer avant sa mort
Que le travail est un trésor.[16]

The textual context in which "Toil and Treasure" was first published is significant both internally and in terms of its links with the other sections of the journal. The section which included the anonymous prose translation of the French fable as well as Bahar's poem bore the heading *Eqterah* (literally, meaning "improvisation," perhaps envisioned more precisely as an impromptu test, presumably of poetic *qariheh* "talent"). Its use, in reference to a section in a literary journal which includes the Persian prose translation of a foreign text and one — or a few — Persian poems based on it, seems to have been initiated by *Daneshkadeh*. Where there were multiple Persian poems composed by different individuals, they all versified the basic idea of the foreign text, yet the participants were apparently free to choose the form, meter, or rhyme scheme of their compositions. [17] Both the word "improvisation" and the multiplicity of contributions suggest a sort of poetic competition among the participants, designed in all likelihood to foster the search for the most appropriate and effective ways of naturalizing European literary texts in the Persian language. The competitive aspect of the practice seems to have become more predominant, since the practice soon became known as *mosabeqeh-ye adabi* (literary competition).[18] It found wide currency in the 1930s

16 La Fontaine, *Oeuvres Complètes*, vol. 1: *Fables, Contes et Nouvelles*, 191.

17 *Eqterah*, a word of Arabic derivation, literally means a test, and is used in this context as a test of poetic talent. Its usage must be seen as an attempt to conceptualize what is involved in terms of the creative process required for it. Of the six times this word is used in *Daneshkadeh*, four refer to Bahar's. versification of a European text.

18 Literary competitions of various sorts were a frequent feature of many early twentieth-century newspapers and journals in Iran. For a particularly interesting one, see *"Jayezeh: Yek ghazal-e Badi'"* (Prize: A Novel Ghazal), *Zaban-e Azad*, no. 33 (October 21, 1917): 4.

and 1940s, although one may still come across instances of it in Iranian literary journals.

In *Daneshkadeh*, this section seems to have grown out of a smaller segment, a filler of sorts, usually placed at the bottom of the pages left partially blank by more extensive essays in the journal. In such spaces, aphorisms from many European literary figures were printed in translation. Aphorisms published in the first issue, for example, bear the names of Schiller, Flammarion, Armant, Bordello, and Victor Hugo.[19] The first time the term Eqterah appears in the journal, it is accompanied by the subhead *Dar Qate'at-e Adabiye Faranseh* [in — or on — French literary fragments]. The section following the heading contains a prose translation of a fragment from Boileau's "Pyrrhus," followed in turn by a composition by Bahar billed as a "versified translation of Boileau's fragment" (*tarjomeh-ye nazmi-ye qet'eh-ye bu'alo*).[20] Such designations are absent from *Daneshkadeh's* later Eqterahs.

Within the section containing La Fontaine's "Le Laboureur ...," Bahar's poem is published after the fable's Persian prose translation, a fact that marks the latter as a preliminary, and necessary, step toward the Persian poet's "improvisation." Because we have no evidence that Bahar had direct access to La Fontaine's fable (we know he did not know much French), we may assume that the stylistic features of the Persian prose translation were significant in informing and constraining his composition. So, let me explore that ground a little. Entitled *"Zare' va Pesaran-e U"* (The Farmer and His Sons), the Persian prose translation is unpretentious, even by the standards of literary translation current at the time. It is printed in regular prose fashion, filling every line, as if it were a story out of a prose collection in Persian; it does not strive for any rhetorical or lexical embellishments or poetic effect in its syntax or diction. It highlights the moral of La Fontaine's fable by setting the Persian translation of the first two lines in bold letters. Thus, *"Travaillez, prenez de la peine: / C'est le fonds qui manque le moins,"* appears in Persian in a way comparable to: **"kar konid va ranj barid in yek sarmayeh-i-st keh hargez gom nakhahid kard."**

Its prosaic diction and style notwithstanding, the prose translation supplies some of Bahar's key terms, such as *ranj* (*la peine*/toil), *ganj* (*trésor*/treasure), *sarmayeh* (*le fonds*/capital) and *miras* (*l'héritage*/heritage). It also provides the lexical basis for some of the poetic phrases, clauses, and patterns

---

19 *Daneshkadeh*, no. 1 (April 21, 1918): 22.

20 Ibid., no. 2 (May 22, 1918): 104–7.

Bahar uses. For instance, in Bahar's poetic phrase *man an ra nadanestam andar koja-st,* one can easily see traces of the prose sentence *man ja-ye an ra nemidanam* (I do not know its place); or a syntactic pattern like *ham inja ham anja va har ja keh bud* (both here and there and wherever there was) is easily traceable to the sentence *inja va anja va hameh ja* (here, there, and all over). Finally, although the two rhyming words of *ranj* and *ganj* occur in the prose translation, the text does not attempt to harness the poetic potential of the two rhyming words, nor does it even show an awareness of it. Bahar, however, uses each word several times, and rhymes them twice, once in the seventh line and once in the final line. In this way, he highlights the ultimate relationship between the concepts those words express. The culture has exploited this potential even more. In successive editions of Bahar's *Divan* — as well as in the textbooks where the poem is published — the two rhyming words have been elevated to the poem's title.[21]

Bahar's additions and omissions of textual entities are no less significant. He gives an affirmative character to the opening moral *sententiae* by changing the clause describing the capital that is work — *keh hargez gom nakhahid kard* (which you will never lose) — into the adjective "eternal" (*javdani*). In doing so, he turns a characterization of work that is negatively phrased into a positive modifier for it. In the episode itself, he omits the reference to the absence of a witness, present in the prose translation as in the French original. In the prose translation, La Fontaine's *leur parla sans témoins* (he told them without [the presence of] a witness) had been translated literally as *bedun-e shahedi beh anha goft* (without a witness he said). However, a subtle shift has occurred in the process. In the original, the word *témoins* rhymes with the *"le moins"* of the opening rhyme, while the concept behind it conveys the privacy of the husbandman's meeting with his sons. The French phrase then contains a poetic allusion. As is common in the case of family secrets and natural to the circumstances of the episode, the husbandman reveals the secret to his sons in private. That link is absent from the prose translation. In Persian, the idea would be phrased more commonly as *dar khelvat* (in private), *mahramaneh* (secretly), or *dur az cheshm-e digaran* (away from the eyes of others). With its legal and jurisprudential undertones, the phrase *bedun-e shahed* (without a witness) communicates a secretiveness more appropriate to a plot being hatched than to a family secret being shared. This is probably due to the emergence of a legal jargon in the

---

21 Bahar (Poetic Divan), 1: 1108. For an example of the textbook reproduction of the poem, see Islamic Republic of Iran, Ministry of Education, *Farsi-e Chaharome Dabestan* (Persian for Fourth-Grade Elementary Schools), 104.

discourse of Iran's modernizing and secularizing culture. The Persian phrase would be more likely to take our attention away from the idea of the lesson that the husbandman wishes to impart to his sons and guide it in unpredictable directions. In other words, even though shahed is a proper Persian equivalent for the French *témoins*, La Fontaine's concept has undergone a change in the process of translation from French verse into Persian prose, giving the translation of character on that point which may have appeared odd, out of place, or even misleading to Bahar. He deletes all explicit reference to the privacy of the meeting, relying on the word *beh farzandegan* (to the sons) to convey the idea.

Examples of culturally significant changes are too many to enumerate. Bahar recedes the reference to the sale of the inherited property, expressing the idea instead in terms of the father's advice to his sons: "love your heritage" (*miras-e khod ra bedarid dust*). He thus guides the concept of the heritage toward greater abstraction, metonymically aligning it with such concepts as "the land," and from there to "the country," or perhaps "culture" of Iran; this concept is more closely aligned with the notion of Iran as the "heritage of Iranians," and accords more intimately with the patriotic discourse of the time.[22] In a conceptually contrary move, he concretizes the image of the activity expected of the sons by turning the prose version's rather abstract and awkward formula qadri esteqamat *az tarafe shoma an ra kashf khahad kard* (some perseverance on your part will unearth it) into *pajuhidan o yaftan ba shoma-st* (to search and to find is up to you). There are other words, too, which he adds in order to make the poem more culturally anchored. Substitutions like *mehregan* for pa'iz (the prose version's rendition of the French word *l'août* [August]), and additions like *dasht* (field), *keshtgah* (plantation), *bagh* (orchard), *gavahan* (plow) realign the poem's cultural axis, make it more specific, or enhance its power to plant an image in the mind of the Persian-speaking reader.

Most significantly, Bahar successfully turns the dictates of rhyme and meter into a source of palpable poetic effects which most visibly distinguish verse from prose in the esthetic culture of his age. Thus, in the first line the repetition of the word *kar* (work) reinforces the message of the fable that work is an important human activity central to the fable's moral. In the second, the *goft/khoft* rhyme helps to express the father's death in terms of sleep, a metaphor for death. And in the third line, the use of the pronoun *u* (he, she) for the land wherein the metaphorical treasure is buried serves

---

22 For an account of Bahar's early political life see Loraine, "Bahar in the Context of Persian Constitutional Revolution." See also Marini, "Bahar."

to personify its referent and classicize the poem. The process culminates in the last two lines where the word *shokhm* (plow), used in the prose translation, is paired with the word *tokhm* (seed) and placed within the proverbial phrase in Persian that metonymically refers to a good harvest. Thus, the hemistich *ze har tokhm bar khast haftad tokhm* (from each seed sprang seventy seeds), while covering the distance between the single seed of the sowing time and the seventy seeds of the harvest, at the same time alludes to the far greater space that separates the surface operations of the prose text to the deep-seated poetic allusions embedded in the Persian language.

As for the French fable's moral, Bahar's manipulation of the Persian prose text seems designed to buttress the lesson he detects in it, while emphasizing the work ethic which he, as a leading member of the Iranian intellectual community, appears determined to instill in the minds of his compatriots. His effort is most clearly visible in the poem's closure where the French fable's identification of work and treasure comes to reiterate the everlasting quality of the capital that is work. Whereas a treasure would be an accidental gain, work is an inexhaustible source of wealth, one that the sons can use to good effect every revolving season. Moreover, whereas no source of knowledge can instruct people in the art of hunting for real treasures buried in the ground, the sons can in turn instruct their offspring in the potential of work to be turned into wealth. All of this, while present in the French fable and its Persian prose translation, is accentuated and buttressed through Bahar's poetic rendition, making La Fontaine's moral far more accessible to the Persian poem's readers. Let us recall, for instance, that the original French fable-and the prose translation-ends with a simple equation: "work is treasure" (*le travail est un trésor/kar kardan ganj ast*). Bahar's poem, in contrast, articulates toil as "becoming" or "turning into" treasure, thus wedding the moral and the fable by highlighting the process rather than the outcome: "their toil ... became their treasure."

One last point merits attention in regard to the moral purport of Bahar's poem. The penultimate line reads thus: *qaza ra dar an sal az an khub shokhm / ze har tokhm bar khast haftad tokhm* (as fate would, that year, for that good tillage / from each seed sprang seventy seeds). In this formulation two forces — fate and human endeavor — are present, both credited equally with the happy outcome of a good harvest. The first, fate, is totally absent from the French fable and, naturally, from the Persian prose version. The translation is very clear on the question of cause and effect here: *pesaran ... be towri khub shokhm kardand keh*

... (the sons ... plowed so well that ...). How do we account for Bahar's addition of "fate"? I can think of two possibilities. First, the term *qaza ra* (as fate would have it) can be seen as a staple of classical Persian verse, used randomly at times as a filler to meet the demands of meter. In this case, Bahar's use of the term would be seen as a stylistic choice thematically unmarked or unsemanticized. The second possibility is that of treating the term as a meaningful lexical entity—that is, one containing some sense. In that case, a problematic relationship arises between the concept communicated through this term and the one conveyed through another semantic unit *az an khub shokhm* (from — meaning because of, or as a result of — that good plowing). What was it that led to the happy outcome, fate or the good plowing? The text is ultimately ambiguous, seeming to want to embrace both readings at the same time. Are we then to take this as a sign of ambivalence in the poetry of a culture in the process of transition from a fact-based notion of life's vicissitudes to one relying more on human endeavor? I have no answer.

Thus, through a complex process of recodification, which includes lexical, rhetorical, and structural additions, omissions, and revisions, the Iranian poet produces a text which, while exhibiting the basic idea of a foreign fable inaccessible to him in all its aspects, changes it formally, generically, and stylistically in ways that consort with his own specific cultural circumstances. The notion of the heritage, it is worth noting, fits Bahar's relatively conservative agenda for literary change and reflects his anxiety about the course of poetic change in Iran, as we have seen in his debates with Raf'at. This concordance between the meaning of La Fontaine's fable and Bahar's efforts to protect the "spirit" of classical Persian poetry from the ravages of excessive modernism would be fully visible when we once again place the poem "Toil and Treasure" in its original context, the literary journal *Daneshkadeh*. There, let us recall, Bahar's poem appeared next to the warnings he issued against undue departures from traditional poetic practice, some of which we saw in the last chapter. Viewed in relation to the criticisms leveled at his pleas for placing poetic change within general considerations of the tradition's continuity,[23] the poem becomes one more statement on the richness of the ancestral field, a case for the necessity of tending the inherited garden and an effective brief against the losses that might result from venturing out.

---

23 Bahar's use of the term *dehqan* is noteworthy. A class of landed gentry, the *dehqans* were thought of at this time as having guarded Iranian identity in the crucial period that followed the Arab conquest of Persia in the seventh century. Ferdowsi, the poet of *Shahnameh*, is identified with this social class.

The relations between Bahar's poem, the prose translation at his disposal, and the French fable on which that translation is based, exemplify certain complex operations at work in the appropriation of already existing textual entities. In all this, "Toil and Treasure" typifies a major type of literary borrowing current in Iranian culture of the early twentieth century. In it, stylistic and rhetorical choices signify the poet's intention to transport as much of the source text's content into his or her own culture by recoding its constituent and structural elements.

Naturally, such a task involves an initial assessment of the foreign text's poetic potential and projections concerning its place in the native literary tradition. Knowing perhaps that he is ultimately dealing with a text which the French culture has classified as "classical," as "verse," and as a "fable," Bahar sets out to produce a text that would fit within the tradition of classical Persian verse fable. Without direct access to all the aspects of the original text, he finds it necessary to rely on the resources of his own language and esthetic tradition as he attempts to poeticize and classicize the Persian prose translation to the extent possible.

Now, Bahar is well known as an excellent versifier capable of vesting a variety of poetic effects in any prose piece. This capability makes it easy not only to see the point on which his versified renditions may differ from their models but also to assign esthetic, cultural, and ideological significance to them. They can be seen, in effect, as manifestations of the poet's intentions rather than as dictates of verse translation. In the case of "Toil and Treasure," at the same time that Bahar's treatment of the theme places the text well within the tradition of verse fables in classical Persian poetry, the poem's didacticism emits a breath of fresh air because the fable itself is new to the system. It therefore introduces a new way of treating a fable, and suggests a novel set of relations between the moral and the anecdote which upholds, exemplifies, and propagates it. Most of the other Iranian versifiers of La Fontaine were forced either to affirm and reinforce his value system or to risk sounding like pale shadows of classical Persian fabulists like Sa'di, 'Attar, or Rumi. In the first instance, their work tends to exhibit signs of rupture with the Persian tradition of verse fable; in the second, they risk losing contact with the foreign text.

Let me turn finally to the reception accorded Bahar's "Toil and Treasure." The manner in which successive generations of Iranian readers have viewed the poem testifies to the presence of an important tendency in that culture. Virtually all traces of the poem's lineage have been eradicated. Certainly, the poet's own heirs seem to have left their patrimony unplowed. Through the five editions of the poet's *Divan*, published since his death under the supervision of his heirs, there is no mention either of the poem's original context in the journal *Daneshkadeh* or of its relationship with La Fontaine's fable.[24] The many biographic accounts and commemorative volumes of the poet's life and works contain practically no reference to those poetic compositions that are modeled on texts of foreign origin.[25] Finally, in the elementary and secondary textbooks where "Toil and Treasure" has been published regularly for the past fifty years or so no mention is made of its origin. This omission has been accomplished so successfully that it has led, at least in one instance known to me, to erroneous attribution. Writing in *Ketab-e Jom'eh*, a journal published in 1979–80, a contemporary scholar of Persian literature has speculated that it may have been a translation from an Arabic poem.[26] The cultural assumption that is working through attempts to conceal the nonnative origins of cherished cultural artifacts ought to be obvious: a poet's stature is diminished if a most celebrated composition of his is found out to have been based on an already existing work. The work could then be called not an original, but a "borrowing." At the cultural level, too, acknowledging literary borrowing is tantamount to undermining the integrity of the national culture. The native zeal for constructing and propagating an imaginary of cultural autonomy works at times through the enforcement of a premeditated — or perhaps not so premeditated — scholarly amnesia.

---

24 In Bahar's *Divan*, the sources of his poems are occasionally identified. In this case, however, no mention is made of La Fontaine's poem or the first context in which Bahar's poem itself was published, this in spite of Bahar's own open attitude as gleaned from the pages of *Daneshkadeh*. Also, in his Divan, attributions are usually phrased in general terms, such as "translation of poems by an English poet" (*tarjomeh-ye ash'ar-e sha'er-e englisi*) or "translation from a French piece" (*tarjomeh az yek qet'eh-ye faranseh*). See Bahar (Poetic Divan), 2: 1087, 110

25 None of Bahar's biographers and commentators known to me has made a reference to the origins of the poem under study here. See Golbon, *Bahar va Adab-e Farsi* (Bahar and Persian Literature); Homa'i, "Takmil-e Sharh-e Hal-e Bahar" (Bahar's Complete Biography); and Matini, "Bahar."

26 See Shamisa, "Malek al-Sho'ara Bahar va Tarjomeh': (Bahar and Translation). This brief note purports to have "discovered" the "source" of Bahar's "Toil and Treasure" to be an Arabic poem entitled "*Al-Fallahu wa Banuhu*" (The Husbandman and His Sons) by the Arab poet Jerjis Hammam, published in a book of juvenile verse entitled *Madarij al-Qira'ah* (Graded Readings), possibly used as a school textbook. In fact, Hammam's is an independent translation into Arabic of La Fontaine's fable, unrelated to Bahar's poem.

An Imagined East
Goethe's Notes and Essays on the *West-Eastern Divan*

Eric Ormsby[1]

In his classic biography of Goethe, Richard Friedenthal remarks of his *The West-Eastern Divan* that '... a supplement containing notes and digressions is appended, but it succeeds only in creating new difficulties, adding new beauties, or providing a bare list of chapter headings of some book he has read.' There is some truth to this description—Goethe does delight in digression—but in most respects it is seriously misleading. The Notes are at once a summation of all that Goethe had learned about Arabic and Persian literature and culture over a long lifetime of serious study as well as an exuberant "invitation to the voyage". Goethe wanted to bring his German readers as close to the "Orient" as he possibly could. Though at first sight, the Notes may appear to be a somewhat loose compendium of scattered facts on everything from Zoroastrianism to the wanderings of the Israelites in the wilderness, with learned asides on Persian and Arab poets and their distinctive rhetoric, including their coded "language of flowers", the work has in fact both a consistency and a cogency all its own. What binds the Notes together is, in the end, not the order and arrangement of the disparate topics but a certain almost indefinable tone, at once light of touch and impassioned. A rare enthusiasm animates, and unites, the Notes. And if I call the work an invitation to the voyage, that is because it is precisely that: Goethe wants to lead his readers into a new and unfamiliar realm, the realm both of the "Orient" as he had come to know it, and that of the *West-Eastern Divan*, a lyrical terrain unlike any other. In this respect, the Notes constitute a vicarious voyage of intellectual discovery, a feat of exploration quite unparalleled in literary history.

1 **Eric Linn Ormsby**, born in Atlanta in 1941, is a poet, a scholar, and a man of letters. He was a longtime resident of Montreal, where he was the Director of University Libraries and subsequently a professor of Islamic thought at McGill University Institute of Islamic Studies. He was Professor and Senior Research Associate at the Institute of Ismaili Studies in London until his retirement in 2013.

In translating the Notes, over an intensive period of two years, I was mainly concerned to capture the spirit of Goethe's prose. The Notes may not always represent Goethe's best prose; they seem sometimes to have been composed in a rush of ebullience and there are disconcerting traces of pedantry. But in general the prose is unmistakably Goethe—at once sprightly and stately. How to convey this without sounding stuffy or pompous? The difficulty lay not only in translating old-fashioned or even archaic words and turns of phrase; that could be resolved by recourse to Grimm's *Wörterbuch* and other earlier reference works. It was, rather, a question of discovering the right, the apt, cadence of the prose. Goethe's language, though German to the hilt, has a slight sheen of foreignness at moments, most notably of French models; in its lightness, its easy elegance, it is faintly reminiscent of his beloved Voltaire. Such effects are not easy to reproduce.

Then, too, I thought it essential to immerse myself as well as I could in the intellectual milieu that Goethe inhabited, particularly in matters relating to Arabic and Persian. To this end I tried to consult as many of the actual editions that Goethe consulted as I could find, whether in English, Latin and German, or in Arabic and Persian. Both the British Library and the library of the Royal Asiatic Society, where I spent many hours over old lithographed editions of Persian chronicles or the original editions of Sir William Jones's pioneering works, came to my rescue. I had the advantage of my academic training in Arabic and Persian in tracking down Goethe's sources but even that did not prepare me for the astonishment I experienced in discovering just how vast and precise Goethe's knowledge of the Islamic world actually was. In my translation I made a point of annotating his references to Arabic and Persian sources. He knew these, of course, from translations into Latin, German, and English. He knew enough of the original languages to become a skilled, if eccentric, calligrapher. More importantly, as certain of his poems demonstrate, he seems to have known how the Arabic and Persian originals sounded. I cannot prove this, of course, but Goethe's inimitable playfulness in the phrasing and the aural effects of many poems in the *Divan* suggest that he had not only read but heard the originals.

As a poet and translator, as well as a lifelong student of Arabic and Persian, I felt quite drawn to Goethe's endeavour in the *Divan* and the *Notes* (which really form a single work)—drawn but also a bit baffled. It seems hardly possible that such a work could be composed today. There is an innocence in Goethe's delight in "the East" that we can probably not recapture. That makes his poems and his comments all the more valuable.

Though he was painfully aware of the discordant elements, even in his imagined Eastern "paradise", he seems to have viewed it all from the vantage-point of Eden, complete with its cloddish "Hans Adam"; there was a purity of perspective in his vision of the East which we are hard put to recreate, let alone recover. Perhaps the two hundredth anniversary, in 2019, of the publication of the *Divan* will freshen our own perspective.

Translating the Notes has prompted me to reflect not only on their contents but on their spirit and I offer certain of these reflections in what follows.

* * * *

Goethe had what might be called an adhesive imagination: it clung to what it loved. And it was capacious enough to encompass entire cultures, even—and perhaps especially—cultures that were alien. At the same time this imagination was no merely passive faculty. It was unusually nimble, mercurial, restless and malleable. It possessed a quickness of adherence. Nor was there anything superficial about this multiple, indeed paradoxical, ability, as is evident throughout all his works, from youth to old age, from *Werther* to *Faust* II. His *West-Östlicher Divan* is probably the supreme example of this assimilative tenacity. And his Notes and Essays on that late collection display just how vast was the range of reference that his shaping imagination adhered to, assimilated, and transformed.

If there was an element of play-acting in his imaginative assimilations, as indeed there was, he was fully conscious of this; he played, with affectionate irony, on that element of make-believe in the poems. And yet that very playfulness had profound and complex sources. Even at his most Olympian, the personal, the private, was ever present, however well hidden even in his loftiest pronouncements. This is abundantly clear in the *Divan*, though his Notes make no reference to the quite personal springs, the intense personal affinities, that animate the poems throughout. Thus, no reference is made to Marianne von Willemer, the thirty-year-old married woman with whom Goethe, then forty years her senior, was passionately in love; and yet, she is the heart and soul of the Book of Suleika (and indeed, she composed several of the poems in that book, though Goethe never acknowledges this openly either in the Notes or in the *Divan* itself). Nor is his young protégé Sulpiz Boisserée ever alluded to even if he arguably played almost as large a role in the composition of the book as had Marianne; it is through Boisserée's own notes and observations, after all, that we know much about the genesis and composition of the *Divan*. And it is Boisserée who is camouflaged in the figure of the "cupbearer" (*Schenker*) in the *Divan*. (Significantly, Goethe kept the two from becoming better acquainted; he feared that "elective affinities" might be sparked between them.)

In the *Divan* Goethe alludes more than once to the paradoxical two-fold mode of vision that was so uniquely his own. The most famous example is the little lyric "Gingo biloba", in many ways the heart of the entire collection:

> *This leaf from an eastern tree,*
> *to my garden entrusted,*
> *for those who savour mystery*
> *has a secret sense when it's tasted.*
>
> *Is it One living thing*
> *that self from self demarcates,*
> *or is it two, the doubling*
> *that a One simulates?*
>
> *I've found a proper reply*
> *to such a question:*
> *Don't you see, in my poetry,*
> *I am both double and One.*

We may be reminded of Faust who exclaims, "Zwei Seelen wohnen ach! in meiner Brust!" but while Faust is divided against himself, the Goethe of the *Divan* encompasses oneness and multiplicity in fruitful simultaneity. Goethe sent the poem with two gingko leaves pasted beneath the text, as a "symbol of friendship", to Marianne von Willemer in 1815 (a copy of the holograph manuscript with the two leaves can be seen at lizzysiddal. wordpress.com). He remarked, according to Boisserée, that "one cannot tell whether it is one divided into two or two that is combined into one". This penchant for twinning himself runs through the entire work. A playful (and celebrated) instance occurs in the poem "Hatem" in which he assumes the voice of Hatim al-Ta'i, an early Arab poet of legendary generosity. In the third stanza he rhymes *Morgenröte* ("dawn") with "Hatem", compelling the reader to substitute "Goethe" to complete the rhyme. Thus he is at once Hatem and Goethe, twin lobes of a single leaf grafted into one. (This, by the way, is but one example of the kind of fun that Goethe had with rhyme elsewhere in the *Divan*. Earlier in the Book of Suleika, again in Hatem's voice, he rhymes "rabbi" with "Mutanabbi", a wild leap of rhyme that brings the greatest of classical Arabic poets into startled conjunction with the rabbinate, a conjunction perhaps only Goethe could have imagined!)

Though he was familiar with translations of Arabic poetry from his adolescence—and with al-Mutanabbi in particular—it was only in 1814 that Goethe first encountered the work of the poet who would come to preside over the entire *Divan* as a tutelary spirit and indeed, even more profoundly, as a double, a brother, a twin, of Goethe himself. This was the great Persian poet Hafiz (ca. 1326-1390) whose *Divan* Goethe read in von Hammer's complete German translation.

Goethe's enchanted engagement with Hafiz may strike us now as a bit strange. There was no question of outright imitation. Thus, Goethe almost never avails himself of the *ghazal*, that old Arabic lyrical form that Persian poets—and especially Hafiz—made so unmistakably their own. The typical *ghazal* is a brief poem of some twelve to fourteen lines with the same rhyme throughout; it usually concludes with a couplet in which the poet addresses himself by the pen-name through which he is known. This device is known by the Arabic term *takhallus* and Hafiz resorts to it faithfully (indeed, "Hafiz" is the pen-name of Shams al-Din Muhammad Shirazi). Goethe prefers the quatrain throughout the *Divan*, not only because it bears some resemblance to the Persian ruba'i, or "four-liner" (best known in the English-speaking world through Edward Fitzgerald's translation of Omar Khayyam), but no doubt also because it lent itself so readily to terse and gnomic expression. The fact that the odd amalgam of Goethe-Hafiz bears little outward resemblance to the actual Hafiz is of no consequence. The *Wahlverwandtschaft*, the "elective affinity", goes deeper than that. It is the spirit of the Persian poet that Goethe strives to assimilate; or perhaps we should say, the spirit of Hafiz as Goethe grasped it. For Goethe, that spirit was at once mocking and melodious, skeptical and devout. It delighted in a sovereign ambiguity. When, for example, Hafiz, the real Hafiz, writes "Last night I saw the angels rap at the tavern door" or when, even more shockingly, he exclaims, "Dye the prayer-mat with wine!" he pushes the bounds of ambiguity to a dangerous extreme. To make matters worse, the tavern is invariably run by a Magian, a Zoroastrian dualist, a *pir-i mughan* in Persian ("a Magian sage") and it is this "arch-heretic" who commands the profanation. What are angels, pure incorporeal beings who stand close to God, doing at a wine-shop in search of a forbidden drink? A distinct whiff of blasphemy suffuses such verses.

This reading of Hafiz persuaded Goethe of the Persian poet's anticlericalism, a stance he admired. It led him even to see Hafiz as a Persian Voltaire, an author he revered (and had translated). The comparison would have astounded Hafiz—and no doubt Voltaire as well. No two writers could be more dissimilar. True, Hafiz does mock and satirize hypocritical Muslim clerics, sometimes very caustically. But this is an old and venerable tradition among Sufis. And it is a satire that subsists within a context of belief. (In this respect, a French writer closer to Hafiz than Voltaire would be Rabelais who lampoons priests and monks within a framework of faith, though Hafiz has none of Rabelais's scurrility.) It is doubtful that Hafiz would have subscribed to the Voltairean "Écrasez l'infâme!" His chosen pen-name of "Hafiz" denotes someone who has committed the entire Koran to memory and Koranic citations and allusions permeate his verse. In his own idiosyncratic way he was deeply pious.

Persian commentators usually interpret Hafiz as writing with a double focus, earthly and mystical. In this reading, such tropes as wine and tavern, rose and nightingale, moth and flame, are to be taken figuratively. After all, for centuries before Hafiz, Sufi poets had used wine to indicate the kind of rapture that the love of God inspires. So the Egyptian Sufi poet Ibn al-Farid (1181-1235) could write "We drank at the remembrance of the Beloved a wine that existed before the creation of the vine." Here the "beloved" is, of course, God, the wine-cup is the Prophet, "remembrance" evokes the Sufi practice of *dhikr*, the ritual chanting of God's name— "remembering Him"—to the point of ecstasy while the wine itself is... what? The rapture occasioned by God's presence, union with Him or something even more utterly ineffable? Wine, the most earth-bound of substances, here becomes something not only of immemorial origin but virtually co-eternal with God; it existed before creation itself. For Goethe, however such shimmering allusion may have attracted him, his wine-poetry remains largely in the anacreontic tradition, itself richly represented in Arabic verse; the 9th-century Arab poet Abu Nawas, a favoured singer at the Abbasid court, is probably its greatest representative. For Goethe, wine is one of the four proper subjects for verse, as he makes plain in both the *Divan* and the Notes. Love occupies pride of place among these subjects, followed by wine, warfare, and "the hateful". In "Elements" he writes, "May love be, above everything, / Our theme when we sing". But the "clink of glasses" (*Klang der Gläser*) and the "clash of arms" (*Waffenklang*) are also noble themes. (In a manner worthy of Hafiz, he plays on derivatives of the verb *klingen* ("to ring, to sound") throughout the poem.)

Goethe's inclusion of "the hateful" or "discontent, vexation" (*der Unmut*), which forms one of the books of the *Divan*, and which he comments on at some length in the *Notes*, deserves comment. The discordant too has its place in the scheme of things. For Goethe this was not only a matter of verisimilitude but it stood in contrast to the prevailing mode and themes of the *Divan*; It accentuated the pervasive tenor of the book, which is one of happiness. The *Divan* is a book of great exuberance but it is also one in which a sovereign delight holds sway—this makes it difficult for us to appreciate nowadays. A happy poet seems a contradiction in terms; we prefer our poets anguished, a bit (or a lot) deranged, riddled by *Weltschmerz*. Goethe certainly had his share of anguish but in his art he strove ultimately for conciliation, for some final triumph of felicity and of serenity, (Even though Goethe called *Faust* a "tragedy", it is really not tragic in the usual sense, as everyone knows and as he himself was the first to acknowledge.) His recognition of an underlying discordance in existence—what W.H. Auden called "the crack in the teacup" that "leads to the land of the dead"—was also an intrinsic aspect of Goethe's doubleness of vision. The bad, the flawed, had to be seen for what it was but it could not be given undue weight; it had to be transcended and overcome.

In "Holy Longing" (*Selige Sehnsucht*), one of the most famous and most beautiful of the poems in the *Divan*, Goethe utters his celebrated admonition "Die and become!" (*stirb und werde!*). According to Max Rychner, in his excellent introduction to the *Divan* (Zürich, 1963), Bertolt Brecht found this statement "banal" but ended up admiring it for its very banality. This typically Brechtian opinion—at once a put-down and a compliment—has a certain pertinence. Goethe's words had always had a rather electrifying effect on me when I read them, as did Rilke's conclusion to his "Archaic Torso of Apollo" ("You must change your life") which echoes Goethe. They embodied a kind of wisdom that could be tucked away in some secret pocket of the mind, a talismanic wisdom. But taken literally, at face value, they do have a ring of the commonplace; the words can seem little more than a summons to "self-renewal" or "self-improvement", the matter beloved of self-help manuals.

Read in the context of Goethe's *Notes*, however, deeper possibilities emerge. In classic Sufi practice from the earliest times, two fundamental stages on the "Sufi path" were known as fana' ("self-extinction") and baqa' (literally, "remaining, continuing"). The Sufi who achieves fana' is one who has annihilated his individual self, not merely his ego but his entire personality; he has become a kind of husk empty of everything but awareness of God. But this is not the final stage; a twofold process is involved. The second stage, that of "remaining", entails a return to the world, a transformed awareness of all phenomena, with newly enlightened eyes. It is possible to understand Goethe's maxim, not merely as some home-spun motto suitable for a sampler, but as a profound and quite urgent imperative. It is a summons to metamorphosis rather than to self-improvement. The moth must be obliterated by flame if it is to assume the splendour of light. The poems in the *Divan* form the vivid record of just such a metamorphosis.

Goethe responded eagerly to the possibilities of a multiplicity of expression that Hafiz's example seemed to embody, and yet, "doubleness" either of vision or of expression isn't quite accurate. The object is rather to write a verse that has a straightforward literal sense but which then expands ever outward in virtually limitless ripples of meaning, the way that the humble plop of a pebble tossed into a pond sends out multiple repercussions of effect in widening rings. When Hafiz writes, "Dark night and frightful wave and whirlpool—how terrifying!" the immediate sense is plain: we are immersed in a night-sea with all its tangible terrors; and when by contrast he evokes "those who cling to the shore" of that sea we have a vivid evocation of utmost dread that is, however, suggestive of much more. Is the night-sea where we drift blindly amid huge waves the world? Or is it the Sufi "ocean of the soul" in which terrified perplexity is the only proper response? Or is it even the realm of divine being itself, which our landlocked vision cannot comprehend? Are there still other ripples of possibility to be discovered in such seemingly plain-spoken verses?

This play of meanings, this playfulness of meanings, is what Goethe strives to emulate in the *Divan*; and in the Notes he takes delight in its possibilities. Sometimes it takes a form of verbal wit. In "Song and Shape", for example (discussed elsewhere here by Joachim Sartorius), the first line reads "Mag der Grieche seinen Thon..." ("May the Greek his clay...") and we are struck by the double resonance of the word Thon. It is "clay" but also, perceptibly, "tone" (Ton) as in music, and this allusive note, so lightly sounded, echoes the contrast between song and shape that is the poem's theme. The example of Persian and Arabic verse seems to have inspired Goethe at the purely verbal level. In those traditions the homely, the bluntly down-to-earth consort quite happily with the lofty, the transcendent, both on the verbal and conceptual levels. Goethe in *Faust* II, could write with reference to Arab women:

> *Recht quammig, quappig, das bezahlen*
> *mit hohem Preis Orientalen...*

Well-upholstered, padded with fat,
Orientals prize their women for that…

Is it going too far to suggest that the odd collocation of the low (presumably colloquial) adjectives *quammig* and *quappig*, with their clotted assonances and alliterations, owes something to the dense aural effects sometimes encountered in classical Arabic verse? I think not for I suspect that such models, once heard, may have tempted Goethe to drive the German language to unexpected "sound effects": the couplet is deftly sing-song—*Knittelvers* and *ghazal* combined—but its vocables positively growl. Certainly no other German poet, before Goethe or after him, has wielded the utmost extremes of the language with such mischievous mastery.

Among the numerous topics that Goethe deals with in his Notes one in particular seems jarring. His discussions of early Arabic poetry, his admiring comments on ancient Persian religious practices, his historical divagations in which even Alexander the Great plays a part (and rightly so, given his place in Arab legend), his sophisticated treatment of Arabic and Persian rhetorical and poetic devices and figures, including his delightful remarks on "the language of flowers", his summaries of accounts of travels to the Orient as well as his tributes to the scholars whose works nourished his—all these appear consistent and fitting to his larger purpose. But why does he include a lengthy excursus on the wanderings of the Israelites in the desert? What do the ancient Israelites have to do with his topic? When we learn that this excursus was something written twenty years earlier and then inserted into the Notes, we may be not only puzzled but irked.

To understand this it is important to keep in mind that in the 19th century the European philological tradition, which Goethe knew well, encompassed a far wider range of subjects than it does today. A specialist in Arabic or Persian or Turkish would have had a firm grounding in Greek and Latin as well as in Hebrew. Biblical studies were in fact the seed-bed out of which Orientalism emerged. Biblical history, biblical exegesis, were central to "Semitic philology" and Goethe shared this conception; indeed, the example of the *Divan* encouraged it among German scholars. Moreover, as Goethe tells us in the Notes, he was from childhood on firmly grounded in the Bible. He was "bibelfest" ("Bible-firm"), as were his predecessors and his contemporaries. He knew the scriptures chapter and verse. This gave him a further affinity with Muslims; in his own immersion in the Bible, he found parallels with those Muslims who had memorized the Koran from an early age. (Such a person was a *hafiz*, the pen-name of his beloved Hafiz). Then, too, the Koran swarmed with Biblical personages—Adam, Abraham, Moses and Pharaoh, Job, Jesus and Mary—all of whom were familiar household presences.

My own teacher, the late S.D. Goitein, the great historian of the medieval Jewish and Muslim world, had been educated in this German philological tradition. He saw the cultures of the Near East as forming a composite culture, despite differences in languages, creeds and customs. For him the affinities between Judaism, Christianity and Islam were greater and more significant than their disparities. Goitein demonstrated this in seminars. When we read early Arabic poetry he would quote comparable passages from the Bible and he did so from memory; he knew the Hebrew Bible virtually by heart. And his quotations were always apt and illuminating, This was the scholarly context within which Goethe, over a century earlier, had written. Nowadays it would be rare for a European or American Arabist to have a command of Hebrew or to draw on Biblical parallels in elucidating Arabic texts. Even an Arabist competent in Hebrew would hesitate to do so today. The discipline has become too disastrously politicized to permit such allusions. In reading the *Divan* and the Notes we can glimpse just how much has been lost.

These works can be seen as part of Goethe's conception of "world literature" but their very specificity, their excitement of tone, at once meticulous and impassioned, set them apart. As his prefatory quatrain announces, they take us into "the poet's land" as well as "the land of poetry". Goethe's own travels never took him to the East but in certain important respects, he not only visited Arabia, Persia and the lands of the Bible but had sojourned there. His is of course, a highly idealized version of "the East". It would have been unrecognizable to an Arab or Persian of his day and to a contemporary Middle Easterner it would appear fanciful, if not preposterous. Nevertheless, in essentials Goethe's vision would have been instantly recognizable to such a reader, and it remains so. For nothing moves and enchants Arab and Persian readers—or for that matter, Turkish, Urdu or Indonesian readers—more than poetry, especially when declaimed or sung. To such a reader Goethe's response to Arabic and Persian poetry would evoke an equally impassioned response. Poetry is as alive and important to such a reader as it was in Goethe's time. The *Divan* is a book that celebrates life in its happiest as well as its saddest aspects, and poetry is the supreme expression of that life.

Goethe, Marianna and the Gingko

Siegfried Unseld

Translated by Kenneth J. Northcott

The date, Friday, 15 September 1815, and the place, the Gerbermühle near Frankfurt, are crucial, not for a large public but certainly for Goethe cognoscenti. Many scholars have described and analyzed the event—Ernst Beutler, Konrad Burdach, Günter Debon, Ernst Grumach, Christoph Perels, Hans-J. Weitz; and I am indebted to Katharina Mommsen for many valuable insights gained from her two volumes of the manuscripts of, and commentaries on, the West-östlicher Divan. On that 15 September 1815, Goethe had joined his friends Johann Jakob Willemer, a banker in Frankfurt and the lessee of the Gerbermühle, his wife Marianne, and Johann Sulpice Boisserée, Goethe's artist friend from Cologne. Goethe had sent a gingko leaf to Marianne Willemer and, with it, the idea "that I am single and twofold."

What preceded this 15 September 1815, and what followed? Nothing less than the period when Goethe's most important poetic work was written, the West-östlicher Divan—the only full-length lyrical work that he himself published during his lifetime . The collection finally appeared in 1819, but on its publication and for a hundred years afterwards it met with relatively little response. It appeared just at the moment when Goethe had more enemies than friends among the literati and those who molded literary opinion. The writers Grabbe and Börne tore the Divan poems to pieces. Heinrich Heine, however, certainly not the most uncritical of poets, recognized their significance: "Goethe has rendered in verse the most intoxicating joie de vivre, and these verses are so light, so happy, so airy, so ethereal that we have to wonder how such a thing was possible . . . , and then Goethe's great thoughts emerge, pure and golden like the stars. The magic of this book is indescribable." Magically too, unintentionally and yet logically, it was a woman and Marianne Willemer herself who stepped into the middle of a book that is both a great work of world literature and a work that, in the light of today's dispute between Western civilization and Islam, gains almost topical significance.

Goethe, consciously and playfully, cloaks the origin of this poetic work in secrecy. At the outset, he still does not know where the poetry will lead him. To the people around him, everything remains secret: the contemporary background, determined by the last days of the Napoleonic Wars, the strong autobiographical nature, and, as the center of thought and feeling, the "little one," the "little woman," Marianne Willemer as muse and initiator, indeed, as co-author.

Because Goethe cloaks his Divan game in secrecy, it is all the more significant that he wants to communicate to his publisher the genesis of the whole undertaking, which forces itself upon him to the point of interfering with an "important piece of business," a new edition of his collected works.

In a letter to his publisher, which he dictated to his secretary Krauter but was never sent, we read: "I have in fact been secretly occupied with oriental literature for a long time and, in order to make myself more intimately acquainted with it, I have written a lot in both the sense and the form of the Orient. In doing this, my intention is to link, in a felicitous manner, East and West, past and present, Persian and German, and to have the mores and modes of thought of both sides overlap one another." Goethe mentions, with thanks, Cotta's gift of the previous year. Gifts from publishers to authors can have consequences! On 10 May 1814, Cotta had, in fact, done Goethe the "favor" of sending him a few "novelties" from his publishing house along with some copies of Cellini that Goethe had asked for. Among these novelties was Der Divan von Mohammed Schemseddin Hafiz. Aus dem Persischen zum ersten Mal ganz übersetzt von Joseph Hammer-Purgstall (The divan of Mohammed Shemedseddin Hafiz, completely translated from the Persian for the first time by Joseph von Hammer-Purgstall, 2 volumes, Stuttgart and Tübingen, 1812–13).

The "favor" served as a catalyst. Goethe recalls the impression that it made on him when he first read it:

> It was last year that I received all of Hafiz's poems in the
> translation by Hammer[-Purgstall], and if previously I had

not taken advantage of the translations of this magnificent poet when they had appeared piecemeal in journals here and there, now as a whole they had all the more lively an effect upon me, and I was obliged to come to terms with them in a productive manner or I should never have been able to hold my own in the face of such a powerful phenomenon. The effect was too vivid, the German translation was at hand, and it was here that I had to find the spur to my own participation. Everything that had been stored away and nurtured in my mind and that bore a similarity either in sense or in substance made its mark, and all the more forcefully, so that I felt an absolute necessity to flee from the real world — which was both an overt and a covert threat — into an ideal world, the participation in which was left to my pleasure, my ability, and my own will.

I have quoted this note in extenso because it is one of the very few documents left in which Goethe discusses his own creative process. Contrary to the great advantages of other poets, there is only one way out for him: he must act productively, accept the challenge as an inducement to participate personally, to create something new out of this spirit.

Here I should mention what Goethe found so fascinating about Hafiz. It was his piety, his vital and erotic power, his sensuality, which made him into a "delightful life's companion" for Goethe. Goethe also admired the masterliness of his poetry. He wanted to set off with Hafiz, to escape. On 21 June 1814 he wrote:

> So Hafiz, may your charming song,
> Your holy example,
> Lead us, as the glasses clink,
> To our creator's temple.

But when he left Weimar with his servant Stadelmann on 25 July 1814, the journey was not to "our creator's temple," nor even "to savor the air of patriarchs in the pure Orient"; it was an escape from the confinement of Weimar, from a marriage that was becoming more difficult by the day, from burdens that fell to his lot in his work as a minister of state (he had to decide, for example, whether deserters from the ducal army should be subject to the death penalty). It was an escape backwards and forwards. Backwards into his former homeland, forwards with a sense of new powers that he drew from nature: it is there that "Phoebus couples with the

Waterfall, a firmament is created, and, as a reassurance — as "a phenom-
enon"— the certainty, "Yes, you will find love."

He arrives in Frankfurt on 28 July 1814. The journey was extremely pro-
ductive: he wrote a number of poems on the way, among them a poem
originally titled "The Book of Sad, Gasele I," then, "Self-sacrifice," then,
"Completion," and finally, in the Divan, "Blessed Longing"; this was a
poem not for the crowd that "scoffs" but for the initiated: "Tell no one,
only the sages." The last two strophes read:

> No distance burdens you too much
> You come flying and enchanted,
> And, at last, desiring light,
>
> You, the butterfly, are burned.
>
> And as long as you do not have it,
> This: Perish and be created!
>
> You are only a melancholy guest
> On this dark earth.

A great poem: "Perish and be created!"—the very heart of the West-
östlicher Divan. It expresses Goethe's idea of the transmigration of souls
("You the butterfly"); his theology of color (the proto-phenomena, light
and dark); "Perish and be created," the resurrection of the dead, the word
of Jesus according to Mark: "Whosoever shall find his life, he will lose
it, and whosoever loses his life for my sake he shall find it." Even Brecht
praises the poem (at Rilke's expense) in his journal (27 October 1940):
"The occasional lapse into the banal, as in the line 'This: Perish and be
created' in the great [sic!] Hafiz poem, simply adds a certain elemental
tone to the whole thing."

Poems like this are written on the journey to Frankfurt and Wiesbaden: at
the end of August the collection has grown to thirty poems. On 4 August
1814, Goethe meets his friend Willemer in Wiesbaden. Johann Jakob Wil-
lemer, born in 1760, raised to the nobility in 1816, was a privy councilor
and senator; grandson, nephew, and cousin of a long line of Lutheran
pastors; and the son and heir of a successful banker. He entered the ser-
vice of the city of Frankfurt in 1790 as an official of the public works
department. In 1792, he was in charge of explosive negotiations with the
French, who were at that time occupying Frankfurt and demanding huge

monetary payments.

On this 4 August, Willemer introduced Goethe fleetingly to a "little companion," Miss Marianne Jung, who would become Goethe's "dear little woman," his Suleika, his soul mate in the Divan, but also the woman for whom he was to develop an immense passion — just as she did for him. Yet they both succeeded in keeping the extent of their intimate relationship secret; only they knew what really happened, and no one should try to decipher the dialogue in "The Book of Suleika" as evidence of a love affair. Goethe did, however, admit in 1819: "Then I really felt that I still belonged to her, the 'dear friend' . . . and so forth, for ever, G."

Who was Marianne? Who was Maria Anna Katharina Theresia Jung? The young woman with the given names of the mother of God, two saints, and Vienna's greatest empress: did she receive these names as protection because she may have been born out of wedlock? We know little of her early life. Miss Jung, who was probably born on 20 November 1784 in Austria, grew up in Vienna. She started acting in 1793—when she was still very young—in the Landstrasse Theater in Vienna; later she had engagements at the theater in Bratislava and then in Baden near Vienna. In 1798 she moved to Frankfurt with her mother.

From 1798 onwards she appeared in the National Theater in Frankfurt, first in the opera The Interrupted Sacrifice and subsequently, after she had also trained as a dancer, in plays, singspiels, and operas. Clemens Brentano saw her in the ballet The Birth of Harlequin and felt attracted to her. In the meantime, Willemer had become chief artistic director of the Frankfurt theater, and Marianne did not escape his notice either. She was not a beauty, but she was attractive and seductive, with a good figure, passionate eyes, and pretty hair. In 1800, Willemer took the actress and dancer as a foster child into his bourgeois establishment, where she was to be educated along with his children, three daughters from his first marriage and a son from his second. Marianne's mother received two thousand guilders and a pension for life, an arrangement she was happy with, and returned to Linz. Marianne had to get used to the new situation on her own, and she made a complete success of it.

Clemens Brentano is a frequent visitor to the house and teaches Marianne the guitar; he falls in love with her. This causes tension between him and Willemer. When there is talk in the Brentano family of a marriage between Marianne and Clemens, Willemer's jealousy gets the upper hand, and he expresses the wish that the two should no longer see one another.

But they meet once more, on 10 May 1802. Brentano writes the poem, "Es stehet im Abendglanze" ("In the brightness of evening, there stands"). After this the relationship breaks up. Willemer now begins to court Marianne himself. He takes care of her education, and seeks to widen her horizons by taking her on journeys to Switzerland and Italy.

Goethe sees her for the first time on 4 August 1814, the day he arrives in Frankfurt. For the sixty-five-year-old Goethe it was a "temporary rejuvenation," a "repetition of puberty," as he explained in his old age during a conversation with Eckermann (11 March 1829), "this can happen to outstandingly gifted people even during old age, while other people are only young once."

Willemer suspects a burgeoning relationship between the two. Marianne cannot conceal her enthusiasm for the poet and can probably not conceal the intense emotional bond that was already making itself felt. On 27 September 1814, just before a second meeting with Goethe, the fifty-four-year-old Willemer marries Marianne. Before the marriage, Willemer and Goethe had a conversation, the contents of which are unknown except for the supposition that Willemer asked Goethe's advice as to whether he should legitimize his relationship with Marianne. It may be assumed that Goethe advised him to do so. If there was anyone who had had experience of the social consequences of an unmarried relationship and, moreover, one in which the partners came from the most divergent social origins, it was Goethe. Of course, he had to recognize an important difference. Willemer—who admitted to Goethe, "I grew up with no education and learned nothing"—had given his adopted daughter, and subsequent paramour, an excellent education. Goethe, whose education was nonpareil, never gave Christiane the chance to acquire an education; he gave her privileges but was of little help to her in the exercise of them. Goethe was to greet the marriage with sober words. Boisserée wrote them down in his diary (3 October 1815): "Thus the salvation of the lovable little woman is a great moral good."

Fräulein Jung lived for eighteen years in Willemer's house before he married her; Christiane Vulpius was Goethe's housekeeper for eighteen years before Goethe finally made her his wife, the wife of a privy councilor and, later, minister of state. Willemer's marriage was extremely hurried; there was no engagement, nor were the banns read. The wedding in Frankfurt between the Lutheran Willemer and the Catholic Marianne was celebrated by Pastor Kirchner of the Church of the Holy Spirit—it was not a church wedding but a private one. Marianne's birth certificate was not produced; nor was her father's death certificate. The papers were supposed to be sent from Linz, where her mother lived, but they never arrived. It was for this reason that Marianne never became a citizen of Frankfurt. She was, and remained, during her sixty years in Frankfurt, a "foreigner." What were to be the words in the Divan?

> You must earn yourself a good reputation,
> Learn to make good judgments;
> Anyone wishing to go further will perish.

Shortly before the marriage, Goethe meets Marianne at the Gerbermühle for the second time. When he sees her for the third time, on 12 October 1814, she is already married to Willemer, "our worthy friend." Goethe is in no hurry to tell his wife Christiane of the marriage. On 12 October, he dictates a letter to his servant Stadelmann intended for Christiane: "In the evening to Frau Geheimrat Willemer, for now our worthy friend is married *in forma*. She is as kind and good as before. He was not at home." A blunt report and with good reason.

In October 1814, Goethe and Marianne meet again in Frankfurt. The nine days in October are an experience for Marianne. On 18 October, they stand on the Mühlberg in Frankfurt and watch the fireworks display celebrating the anniversary of the Battle of Leipzig. Goethe made a note of the day; for Marianne it would remain an existentially crucial day, to which she returned again and again.

Goethe also writes about his last day in Frankfurt in his diary: "Visits, Marianne; . . . left at about two o'clock." On 20 October, Goethe begins his return journey to Weimar. He was not to see Marianne again until the summer of 1815. The two remain in a complicated, somewhat conspiratorial, relationship, through friends, through Willemer's daughters, through letters, indeed even through Goethe's encoded letters to Willemer. Then through poems by Goethe and by Marianne. He always addresses her as "dear little one" although he does talk over and over again in jest, but half seriously, of "little Blücher," "little critic," "little Don Juan."

On 12 December, Willemer reminds Goethe that he owes them some sign of his continued existence: "Since you started calling my wife 'little one' she simply refuses to grow up any more, except in her heart." Two days later Goethe reacts: "I have not forgotten that I owe the dear little one some sign of life," and he sends a poem, the last strophe of which reads:

And thus from afar
This page brings you golden words,
Even though the characters are black
Your affectionate look will gild them.

The summer months of 1814 were extremely productive for Goethe. He wrote several poems. They constituted, as he told Riemer on 30 August, "a little whole, which can probably expand if my state of mind grows active again." It remains active. Goethe finds a new title for what until then had been known as Poems to Hafiz; now they are called Deutscher Divan (German divan). With this title Goethe has found a central concept. He is ready to try once more—notice the claim—"to measure our private circumstances against the terrible yardstick of world history." He sees his personal experience (he describes it as "sorrow, fear, apprehension, terror, and suffering") against the background of the political events of these years, years in which one epoch came to an end and another began, in which Napoleon rose and fell, in which the Holy Roman Empire ceased to exist, and in which an attempt was made to establish a new order of peace. Thus, the poems of the Divan became for him a "vehicle of his political credo." How sadly mistaken are those people who would place Goethe in an ivory tower and call him apolitical, someone who fled from reality.

In May 1815, Goethe organizes the hundred poems that he has written so far. He believes that the Divan is finished. But it still lacks the "notes and essays" that he meant to include in order to increase the reader's understanding.

Whoever wants to understand poetry
Must enter the land of poetry;
Whoever wants to understand the poet
Must walk around in the poet's land.

On 24 May 1815, Goethe leaves Weimar for Wiesbaden; he goes via Frankfurt, but he does not see the Willemers and is in no hurry to see them again. En route, and in Wiesbaden, he continues to work on the Divan; he writes poems that he will later add to "The Book of Love"—which he had already planned—and the "Book of Suleika," and on 24 May 1815, he writes the lines:

Now that you are called Suleika
I should also have a nickname.

When you praise your beloved,
Hatem, that's the name to use.

Thus, Goethe has given himself a nickname, but he is not referring to Marianne here as Suleika (as Hans Pyritz, one of the first to interpret the poem, in 1941, believed to be the case)—not yet, at least. At that time Marianne was, and remained, his "dear little one" who was always remembered with a greeting.

According to Goethe in his Daily and Annual Notebooks, it was announced in Wiesbaden on 21 June that the battle of Waterloo (18 June 1815) "had been lost, arousing great terror, which then gave way to astonished, indeed stupefying, joy when it was announced that it had been won."

The following six weeks were those that Goethe was later to describe as the "loveliest time."

Things began at the Gerbermühle, a country residence immediately to the southeast of Frankfurt that Willemer had leased for his lifetime. In his "Observations" Goethe calls it a "most pleasant spot." Marianne spoiled him. She describes the daily ritual: In the morning, Goethe was on his own; at noon he appeared in a frock-coat; in the afternoon he liked to go for a walk; he was at his most amiable in the evenings, when he appeared in his white flannel robe and read poems aloud, mostly poems from the Divan collection; his taste in food was "simple," with a marked preference for artichokes. He had brought some wine, which he would drink from a silver goblet that he had also brought with him, at ten o'clock in the morning while eating his lunch. Marianne later summed up her memories of these days (to Hermann Grimm, 12 May 1852): "Goethe, oh! if you only knew him! If you were sitting face to face with me I could probably tell you things about him that not everyone knows: when the rays of his intellect were concentrated in his heart, that was a moment of illumination that called for a particular vision—it was like moonlight and sunlight, one after the other, or even simultaneously, and out of this the wonder of his being became manifest, his awareness, the clarity of his expressions, and the way he brought others to a true, but transfigured, understanding. Enough!"

When Goethe meets Marianne on 12 August, he has Hafiz's (the Persian poet's) Divan for her in his luggage — once more it is to be a momentous gift. For Goethe, the evening is especially pleasing. Marianne picks up the guitar, an instrument strung with eight rather than the usual six strings, which had been bought in Naples during a trip to Italy and still exists. Boisserée's diary tells us what she liked to sing: "Give me your hand, beloved" (Là ci darem le mano), "The God and the Bayadere" (Der Gott und die Bajadere), "Mignon's Song" (Kennst du das Land?), "Oh give from some soft pillow" (O gib vom weichen Pfühle), as well as Austrian folk songs—for she was, according to conjecture, a child of Vienna and herself "a little Don Juan." The heyday of the West-östlicher Divan, the Hatem-Suleika game, has already begun. On this day, Goethe writes mysteriously and evocatively in his diary, "Divan. Beginning—End." What can he have meant? Is "Beginning and End" that important, most important, part of the Divan, the antiphonal exchange between Hatem and Suleika? An antiphony that becomes increasingly a poetic dialogue between Goethe and Marianne. She, Marianne, who ("You now love me too") is to be Suleika and "to me shall always remain Suleika."

Goethe stays with the Willemers in their town house, "the Red Mannikin," from 8 to 15 September. The evenings are spent mainly at the Gerbermühle. He spends a lot of time with his friend Sulpice Boisserée, with whom he visits art exhibitions and goes on trips to Mainz. Goethe's remark about his place of birth, "Frankfurt is chock full of curiosities," dates from this time.

Boisserée has kept a careful record of their conversations up to the evening of 15 September 1815. The themes: Observations of Roman antiquities. Have we lived before? Is there such a thing as transmigration of souls? Pantheism, monotheism, expansion and contraction. There is discussion about Goethe's doctrine of the polarity of all being, of systole and diastole.

On Friday, 15 September, Goethe again accompanies Boisserée from Willemer's town house to the Gerbermühle. Again they talk about art. Boisserée, a Catholic, believes in the Christian content of art; Goethe, in the aesthetic substance. Boisserée discovers the image of the pointed Gothic arch, in which two sides meet at one point. Does this, once again, strengthen Goethe in his concept of the single and the twofold?

In his diary entry for the same day, Boisserée describes the evening of 15 September in the Gerbermühle, a "cheerful evening": "We were sitting on the balcony in the beautiful, warm evening air. Marianne is singing with great feeling and expression." We know the event that set the tone for the whole evening: Goethe had given Marianne a Gingko leaf that he had plucked that afternoon from a Gingko tree (probably in the Brentano Park) and he had written some verses for the occasion, one "verse" of which ran, according to Boisserée, "that I am single and twofold too." Throughout the evening, the assembled company kept returning to this "verse." Boisserée tells us: "G. had sent the Wilmer woman a leaf from the Gingko-biloba in the city as a symbol of friendship. It is not known whether it is a leaf that divides itself into two or two that unite into one. That was the content of the verse." Katharina Mommsen and Hans-J Weitz also assume that by "verse" Goethe meant the whole of the second stanza of the later poem "Gingko biloba." In any case the whole company kept returning to the phrase "I am single and twofold."

But Goethe and Marianne—and they alone—knew something else on that evening. On 12 September, that is, three days earlier, Marianne had received a poem from Goethe, the first poem addressed directly to her. Above it is written "Hatem," the name Goethe gives himself.

Portrait of Goethe by Ferdinand Jagemann

Hatem

It is not opportunity that makes a thief,
For it itself is the greatest thief,
Because it stole what was left of the love
That still remained in my heart.

It handed it over to you,
The sum of all my fortune,
So that now, penniless,
I depend on you alone for sustenance.

Yet already, in the jewel of your glance,
I feel your mercy
And enjoy, within your arms,
A destiny that is renewed.

Goethe, the sixty-six-year-old, empathizes with the youthful poet Hatem;
he feels "the exhilaration of spring and the heat of summer." Marianne is
his Suleika, the Suleika of the "Book of Suleika" that he is to write later.
"You shall always be Suleika to me."

The joy of life is great,
But joy in living greater
If you, Suleika, bring me
Wild delight . . .

Goethe's poem is a single, unambiguous declaration. He speaks of the
"sum of all his fortune" and says that only she can be his "sustenance"
and that he enjoys a "renewed destiny." Goethe, the man of experience,
here emerges from himself, and no doubt he can guess what is happening
to Marianne, a woman who has for all her life remained unfulfilled in her
emotions and now sees fulfillment in the man she loves. But Goethe is
not just the lover; he is the poet who writes, who creates, who, in other
words, is both single and twofold. Poetic form is always distanced from
concrete experience. And he feels "mercy in the jewel of her glance." We
who live today have to recognize that Goethe was always a splendid stage
manager of the work of art that was his own life, that he recognized the
great advantage that his creative muse brought him, but that at the same
time he factored in the breakdown—so necessary for him—of a relation-
ship, of the love of two people who were tied to others, indeed to the
point of including it in the whole scene.

Marianne, and this is the miracle of her existence, replied four days later with a poem that clearly returns the love that is offered her, and demonstrates in it a poetic power that does honor to the recipient. And with this poem she returns a rather unusual word to the German language, emphatically, at the very beginning, hochbeglückt (highly favored). Did she take this epithet from "Wilhelm Meister's Theatrical Mission," where it is sung by the harpist as a response to Wilhelm's request that he should put his trust in him?

This marks the beginning of the poetic exchange between Marianne and Goethe. On 16 September, a Saturday, Marianne writes for Goethe:

Suleika

Highly favored in your love,
I do not scold opportunity.
If to you it was a thief,
How glad am I for such a theft.

And in any case why rob?
Give yourself to me of your free will
Gladly, oh! too gladly, would I believe
That I am she who stole from you.

What you have so willingly given
Will bring a handsome reward,
My peace, my rich existence,
I give you gladly, take it.

Do not jest, don't talk of poverty.
Does not love enrich us both?
If I hold you in my arms
There is no greater joy than mine.

The master accepts the evidence of her homage, makes a few corrections to the text, copies it, and puts it with the other manuscripts. The manuscripts—dated 17 September—are later to be incorporated into the dialog in the "Book of Suleika," a dialog that also emanates from Marianne: "When I was sailing on the Euphrates . . ." and Hatem's answer: "I am willing to interpret this!"

Goethe replies and acts like an author. But he cannot ignore, at least after the poem "Highly favored in your love," what he has done to Marianne. She loves him with every fiber of her being. This is how the duodrama begins, and Goethe responds as he always does to situations that he regards as hopeless, by taking flight. On 18 September 1815, he leaves the Gerbermühle and leaves Frankfurt. He hastens to Heidelberg to confer with some famous orientalists, "learned men." He tells the Willemers that he will not be returning via Frankfurt. But what he could not know was that the Willemers would show up in Heidelberg, unannounced and unexpected, on 23 September. Marianne could not bear not to see him again. Goethe takes Marianne into the castle grounds and shows her the Gingko tree there. After sending the leaf and after the evening in the Gerbermühle, this is now the third time that Goethe draws her attention to the Gingko tree and explains the "secret meaning": "Is it one thing that divides into two, or two that unite in one?"

On their final day together, on 26 September, the Willemers and Goethe are walking through the park. He takes Marianne aside and leads her to the fountain. Then he writes the name Suleika in the sand, in Arabic characters (which he had learned the previous day from one of the "learned men," the orientalist Heinrich Eberhard Gottlob Paulus). The Willemers leave Heidelberg, still hoping that they will see Goethe again. But he knows differently. He knows that there cannot be another meeting. In his diary for 25 September, we read, "Evening, music, conversation, farewell." On 26 September, "Departure of the friends. Divan. Stayed at home." Marianne was never to see Goethe again. He himself is filled with emotion. His heart pounds. In his desperation he immerses himself in Persian studies, visits Professor Creutzer, talks to him about the pregnant symbolism and ambiguity of the ancient myths. Every form, according to Creutzer, has a double meaning. Goethe remarks, "Rather like this leaf then, single and twofold."

Then, in a mood of final farewell, of separation from a love that he is sacrificing so that he can continue his work—continue his "poems"—he writes the poem that is later called "Gingo biloba." He sends it to Frankfurt on 27 September. He does not address it directly to Marianne, although she has to be seen as the only truly intended recipient, but sends it to her friend, and Willemer's daughter, Rosine Städel. He explains that he has written a "rhythmic translation, in other words a poem," as an addition to the prosaic explanation he had given of the "well-known, wonderful" leaf on that earlier evening in the Gerbermühle.

There are three versions of the poem which, it is true, vary only in minor ways from one another; but because even the most trivial deviation adds to the way the poem can be interpreted, all three versions are quoted here in the original.[1]

Version 1: the poem that Goethe sent to Rosine Städel for Marianne:

Dieses Baums Blat, der, von Osten,
Meinem Garten anvertraut,
Gibt geheimen Sinn zu kosten,
Wie's den Wissenden erbaut.

Ist es ein lebendig Wesen?
Das sich in sich selbst getrennt;
Sind es Zwey? die sich erlesen,
Dass man sie als Eines kennt.

Solche Frage zu erwidern
Fand ich wohl den rechten Sinn;
Fühlst du nicht an meinen Liedern,
Dass ich Eins und doppelt bin?

This tree's leaf, which, from the Orient,
Is entrusted to my garden,
Lets us savor a secret meaning
As to how it edifies the learned man.

Is it one living being
That divides itself into itself?
Are there two who have chosen each other,
So that they are known as one?

To reply to such a question
I found, I think, the condign sense.
Do you not feel that in my poems
I am single and twofold?

Version 2: As Günther Debon pointed out, this is the well-known man-uscript, an enclosure in a letter to the grand duke Carl August on 10 March 1820, that Katharina Mommsen reproduces in her collection of documents pertaining to the Divan: "Your Majesty receives with this the

---

1 Translator's note: I am quoting the original of all three versions before my translation, as reference is made to rhymes and other elements that cannot be reproduced in English.

promised dispatch from Vienna. . . . (2) 'On the Gingko,' by Freiherr von Jacquin."

Goethe follows the scientific practice of taking over the name introduced by Linnaeus. The date cited here by Goethe, "15 Sept. 1815," is not the day on which the poem was written but a reminiscence of the evening in the Gerbermühle, which for Goethe was the seed from which the poem grew.

Gingko biloba

Dieses Baums Blatt, der, von Osten,
Meinem Garten anvertraut,
Giebt geheimen Sinn zu kosten,
Wie's den Wissenden erbaut.

Ist es Ein lebendig Wesen?
Das sich in sich selbst getrennt;
Sind es Zwey? die sich erlesen,
Dass man sie als Eines kennt.

Solche Frage zu erwiedern
Fand ich wohl den rechten Sinn;
Fühlst du nicht an meinen Liedern,
Dass ich Eins und doppelt bin?

Gingko biloba

This tree's leaf which from the Orient
Is entrusted to my garden
Lets us savor a secret meaning
As to how it edifies the learned man.

Is it one living being?
That divides itself into itself
Are there two who have chosen each other,
So that they are known as one?

To reply to such a question
I found, I think, the condign sense.
Do you not feel that in my poems
I am single and twofold?

Version 3: The first printing of the poem in the edition of the book entitled, *Der west-östliche Divan*, published in 1819.

Gingo biloba

Dieses Baum's Blatt, der von Osten
Meinem Garten anvertraut,
Giebt geheimen Sinn zu kosten,
Wie's den Wissenden erbaut.

Ist es ein lebendig Wesen?
Das sich in sich selbst getrennt,
Sind es zwey? die sich erlesen,
Dass man sie als eines kennt.

A page from the first printing of the *West-östlicher Divan*, 1819

Solche Frage zu erwiedern
Fand ich wohl den rechten Sinn;
Fühlst du nicht an meinen Liedern
Dass ich Eins und doppelt bin?

The gingko, that Eastern tree,
In my garden plot now grows.
In its leaf there seems to be
A secret that the wise man knows.

Is that leaf one and lonely?
In itself in two divided?
Is it two that have decided
To be seen as one leaf only?

To such questions I reply:
Do not my love songs say to you
– Should you ever wonder why
I sing, that I am one yet two?[2]

In his letter to Rosine Städel, Goethe plays his Divan game: "I am sending you with this letter, dear Rosette, the poem with all the secrets of modern philology, my own as well, for whatever private use you would like to make of them." This hint, taken together with reference to the origin, to the conversations in the Gerbermühle, to Heidelberg, to the position occupied by the poem in the "Book of Suleika" allows us to interpret it in two ways—erotically as well as a poetico-hermeneutically—and this has a bearing upon Goethe's works, his poetry, as a whole.

The poem, in three stanzas of four lines, each line consisting of four trochees, forms the theme of the writer's appointed task. The first stanza asks about the "secret meaning" of the "tree's leaf" (Baumes Blatt), a striking deictic alliteration. The second stanza lays out, as a riddle, the paradox of unity and duality. Then, in the third stanza—as an answer to the "secret meaning"—the "condign sense," the solution to the riddle.

But real life is interwoven into all stages of the poem. Two lovers become one in the act of love, and yet Hatem knows, Goethe knows, that unity is always conditioned by duality. Just as the leaf, which Goethe sees as

---

2 This rhymed rendition of the poem was added to the essay where Kenneth Northcott only repeated his literal translation of the original – version 2 above. This rendition was done by Anthea Bell and is reproduced in this volume with the author's permission.

wanting to divide, actually does divide, revealing the unity in the duality. Two as one? To reply to "such a question" is the meaning of the poem. It is not chance that bin ("am") and Sinn ("meaning") correspond as a rhyming pair. And Hatem's—Goethe's—answer is immediate. With the simple trochaic line scheme (Greek trochaios = runner), simple short rhymes, reflexive or even prosaic constructions that are scarcely embellished with adjectives and lack Goethe's usual colorfulness, Goethe goes full tilt to the last line: reader, do you not feel, Marianne, do you not feel in what I write "that I am single and twofold?"

He is the lover and the beloved, but at the same time he is the poet who lives in his songs, his poems, his works. Does he exist only in his poems? Not as lover and beloved? Is he, in this way, "single and twofold"? The I, the subject, and the he, the object, of his poem.

She too is lover and beloved. But whereas Goethe, directing the strategy of the work of art that is his life, knowing the principle of distance when he finds himself in extreme situations, recoils from commitments, shuns them, "goes away from them" in the truest sense of the words, renounces them, yet is always ready for new experiences, as when, at his midday meal in Hardheim on his return journey on 7 October, he sees and kisses a "fresh young girl," Marianne, for her part, is in despair, plunges into sickness and depression. She had not recognized the part that imagination played in what Goethe had brought to her, and could therefore not respect the borderline between fiction and reality. He had raised her to the star of stars as Suleika, and so her fall was all the greater when Goethe went out of her life.

But we have not reckoned with one essential factor. When Marianne arrived in Heidelberg and surprised Goethe there, she handed him this poem, which she had written on the way:

Suleika

What does this emotion mean?
Does the east wind bring glad tidings?
The fresh motion of its wings
Cools the heart's deep wound.

Its caress plays with the dust,
Stirs it up in little puffs,
Drives the little crowd of insects
To the vine's secure bower.

Gently the sun's fierce heat softens
And cools my glowing cheeks as well,
And kisses, in its fleeting course,
The grapes resplendent on field and hill

And its gentle whisper brings me
A thousand greetings from my friend,
Even 'ere these hills grow darker
A thousand kisses rise to greet me.

And so you may go on your way,
Serve your friends and those who grieve,
There where high walls glow and glisten
I soon shall find the one I dearly love.

Ah! the true, the heartfelt, message
Breath of love, and life refreshed,
Comes but from his mouth alone,
His breath alone can give me that.

Only a few days later a poem to the "west wind" follows the "glad tid-ings" of the east wind, as she leaves Heidelberg expressing her sorrow at the parting.

Suleika

Ah! west wind how I envy you
Your dampened wings,
For you can bring him tidings
Of my suffering at our parting.

The movement of your wings
Awakens a quiet longing in my breast,
Flowers, eyes, woods, and hill
Stand weeping with your every breath.

Yet your mild and gentle wafting
Cools the aching eyelids:
Ah! with sorrow I would perish,
Had I no hope of seeing him.

Hasten to my love then,
Speak softly to his heart,

But take care not to make him sorrow,
And keep my pains concealed from him.

Tell him, oh! but tell him gently,
That his love is now my life,
That his presence will afford me
A joyous feeling of them both.

These are two wonderful poems, in the spirit both of Goethe's verse and of Hafiz's (in which Marianne, wonder of wonders, had so quickly and deeply immersed herself). They are poems equal to Goethe's in merit and, in this case, perhaps even exceed Goethe's in their warmth and devotion.

It is astonishing how well Marianne learned the art that Goethe, in his Notes and Essays, describes under the rubric "Cipher": "It happens when two people agree upon a book and when they make page and line numbers into a letter and are certain that the recipient will, with only a small expenditure of effort, understand the meaning." In these coded poems by Marianne, there are individual lines and verses from poems by Hafiz and Goethe that are so artfully composed that, beyond the declaration of love and beyond a poetic game fraught with meaning, beautiful lyrics are born. When Goethe realized the depth of feeling and the art of the poetry, he was deeply moved. He reacted in a "twofold" manner. First, during his days in Heidelberg, he himself wrote poems that number among his finest. One was "Reunion," for Goethe had unexpectedly found Marianne again: once more the Gingko-biloba theme of the one in two, of being torn apart and then finding one another again; but the poem refers not only to love but to the whole world: the world is created out of the division of light and darkness. Then there is a poem in which Hatem sings, "Your locks make me your prisoner!" and "an Etna erupts before you!" In this poem Goethe, who usually conceals everything, gives us what almost amounts to a revelation.

Like the blush of dawn
You shame the somber rampart of those peaks
And once again . . . feels

Du beschämst wie Morgenröte
Jener Gipfel ernste Wand,
Und noch einmal fühlet . . .

Now according to the rhyme scheme, the name "Goethe" (rhyming with Morgenröte) should follow the word fühlet (in German, the subject and verb are reversed here), but the stanza continues without a rhyme, though significantly, with *Hatem*

> *And once again Hatem feels*
> *The breath of spring and summer's heat.*

Goethe pastes the fair copy of the poems "East Wind" and "West Wind" into the original manuscript of the Divan, where the poem "Highly favored in your love" has already found a place.

Goethe never returned to his childhood home. On his journey to the Rhine in July 1816, he said expressly that he did not wish to visit his hometown ("I shall travel via Würzburg, so as not to make contact with the divided city of Frankfurt at this moment"). But the axle of his carriage broke, and he had to remain in Thuringia.

The Divan appeared in 1819. As we have already mentioned, it was not an undisputed success when it first appeared; first editions were still to be found in German bookstores a century later. But then the significance of this great lyric work started to be generally accepted. Felix Mendelssohn, Franz Schubert, and Robert Schumann set the poems to music, and they have entered the treasury of German song.

Marianne kept up a sporadic correspondence with Goethe. On 25 August 1824, she sent him a letter from the Gerbermühle "for your birthday." "The Main is dark blue, the clouds almost green, and the hill is violet, just as it was then, but one person who looks at it, interprets it, and in this way gives pleasure to others, is missing. . . . Remember me with love, and may what follows give proof that I remember you." A poem was enclosed with the letter.

Heidelberg Castle

28 July at seven o'clock in the evening

> *I greet you light-bejeweled rooms,*
> *You ancient, richly garlanded princely edifice,*
> *I greet you, lofty trees, thick with leaves,*
> *And, over you, the deep blue of the heavens.*

Where'er the eye casts its searching glance
In this blossom-laden, peaceful place,
A greeting from my lover, softly spoken,
comes to me From my life's most joyous dream

Once he would come and go upon the
Parapet around this terrace;
I looked for the signs, the gage of true devotion,
I looked and cannot see them.

There is that tree's leaf, that from the distant East
Was entrusted to the west-east garden.
It lets me savor a secret meaning
That edifies the one who loves.

The lofty north wind marched through that hall,
Threatening our peaceful lot,
The rude proximity of warrior hordes
Deprived us of the fleeting moment.

From the cool fountain where the pure spring
Rushes o'er the green-enhaloed marble steps,
Wave after wave comes not more softly, quickly,
Than the words and glances that are here exchanged

Oh, weary eyelids close!
In the twilight of that joyous time
My beloved's lofty poems encompass me
With their tones, and now the past becomes the present.

Weave, O you evening breezes, a golden web
Of sunbeams round this magic place;
Intoxicate me, take me away, you floral scents,
Your power casts a spell, I cannot leave.

Surround me, you invisible barriers,
In a fairy circle, magically,
Sink down willingly thoughts and senses,
Here I was happy, loving and beloved.

We hear the nearness to the Gingko poem, to its creator, and we feel the happiness that has escaped the seventy-five-year-old: "I was happy here, loving and beloved." Ernst Beutler, a great Goethe scholar, once wrote: "These three poems by Marianne, the one to Heidelberg and the ones to the winds as messengers of love, are the most beautiful poems ever written by a German woman." Such praise is fulsome, and differences can certainly be found between the two east-west poems and this last one to Heidelberg, but there can be no question that they are important poems, and that the woman who wrote them was a poet.

The antiphony of the Divan is unique in the history of literature. There are, of course, the great (literary) lovers and beloveds, Beatrice, Laura, Diotima; there are poetic antiphonies like that of Ausonius and Paulinus von Nola; but there are few examples of male and female communal production at the highest poetic level.

On 10 February 1832, Goethe was preparing to send back the letters that he had collected.

> While I am making serious use of the time that is still left to me, the endless papers that have collected around me, so as to look through them and determine what to do with them, certain letters pointing to the loveliest days of my life shine forth: many of this sort have been separated from the others

A watercolour and ink drawing by Goethe of the
side terrace of Heidelberg castle, 1820

for a very long time, but now they are packed up and sealed. A packet of this sort lies in front of me now, bearing your address, and I would like to send it to you at once, in or- der to avoid any accidents. I would only ask for one promise, that you leave it unopened for an undetermined time. Let- ters of this sort give us the happy feeling that we have really lived: these are the most beautiful documents upon which we may rest.

On 29 February 1832, Goethe sent off the following poem, which he had written in 1831, along with the sealed packet containing her letters:

Frau Geheimrätin von Willemer, Your Grace

Frankfurt am Mayn.

These pages shall now travel
To the eyes of my beloved,
To the fingers that once wrote them —
In the hottest of desire
Awaited as they were received—
To the breast from which they sprang,
Always loving, always ready,
Witness to the loveliest of times.

Weimar, 3 March 1831. J.W. v. Goethe

This is the arc that stretches from 1814 and the Suleika year 1815 to the year of Goethe's death, when he makes his statement about the "loveliest of times." We have to wonder, when he was addressing the letters to "the fingers that wrote them," whether he was thinking of the poems of the Divan as well.

A final echo from the autumn of 1860. The seventy-six-year-old Marianne wishes to take another trip from the Gerbermühle to Heidelberg. She does so, and she stands in the castle garden at the fountain, where Goethe had written her name in the sand. She describes the scene: "This is where he kissed me. . . . This is where he wrote a line of verse in the sand with his cane." And of the Gingko tree she says, "This is the tree he brought me a leaf from" (when he met her at the Gerbermühle). She reveals to her companion something that no one but Boisserée and Hermann Grimm knew at the time, that she was the Suleika of the Divan, "but the world knows nothing of that, and now there is no need for everyone to find out."

Goethe's Divan appeared in the autumn of 1819: *West-oestlicher Divan. Von Goethe.* Stuttgard in der Cottaischen Buchhandlung 1819. With a copper-engraved frontispiece and an engraved title page (of Goethe's own design). The volume contains Marianne's three poems almost unaltered, "Highly favored in your love," "What does this emotion mean?" and "How I envy you your dampened wings!" as well as the poem that Marianne said "was on her conscience": "Tell me, you must have written a lot of verse?" She probably inspired other poems or passages as well.

Goethe gives no reason for including these poems in the volume or for his failure to mention that they were written by Marianne Willemer. Of course, he could assume that a small circle of friends knew of his relationship with Marianne and thus of the autobiographical background to the antiphony between Suleika and Hatem. But only the two of them knew that the poems had been taken over verbatim. The secret was kept until 1869.

On 22 August 1819, Goethe sent an advance copy of the Divan to Willemer: "I have received the final copies so late that I cannot even get them bound." When the bound copies arrived in November, Goethe sent one to Marianne and enclosed the following lines:

> *Oh, my darling, the poems unfettered*
> *Squeeze into a rigid volume.*
> *Poems that, in the purity of heaven,*
> *Flew happily hither and yon.*
> *Time spoils everything,*
> *They alone preserve themselves*
> *Every line shall be immortal,*
> *As eternal as love itself.*

> *1815   1819*

Certainly a sensitive dedication. But could he not have mentioned more explicitly here, and to Marianne, the poems that were totally hers, and perhaps have thanked her for them? The "unfettered poems," that "flew hither and yon" are surely too subtle a hint. To Willemer he wrote of the Divan volume: "Meanwhile, may the past step up into the present, and may the friend grow as close as possible." Goethe spoke to Marianne about her poems on only one occasion. In the book Beiträge zur Poesie

(Essays on poetry), he told her, these were precisely the poems that Eckermann had mentioned, giving pride of place to the verses on the west wind. "How often have I heard the song sung," wrote Goethe to Marianne on 9 May 1824, "how often heard its praise and, in silence, smilingly took as my own, what could indeed, in the sweetest sense, be called my own."

"In the sweetest sense my own." What is this sweetest sense? He could feel that he was the initiator; he alone inspired Marianne to write these poems. She had written occasional poems for birthdays and family celebrations before the Suleika year of 1815, and she went on to write poems after that year, but never a poem of such dignity and poetic worth. Is this the "sweetest sense" that allowed Goethe to call the poems "his own"? Marianne describes her situation, at length, in a letter to Goethe in October 1819.

> It is always a difficult task to send thoughts and words from afar to someone far away, when such thoughts only flourish when you are close together; the heartfelt feeling either expresses itself completely or not at all, and when we say "An eloquent silence often tells you more than an eloquent tongue," that assumes that there is a pleasing closeness. If I use these general observations to describe my situation, then it follows that I should really remain silent, but, compelled to speak by the distance that separates us, I will try to see whether I can unite both in writing.

> I have read the Divan over and over again: I can neither describe nor explain to myself the feeling that gripped me as I read every related note of it; if my being and my inner self became as clear to you as I hope and wish and, indeed, may be certain that they did — for my heart lay open to your gaze — then there is no need to go on describing it, for it would, in any case, be a highly inadequate description. You feel and know exactly what was happening to me; I was a puzzle to myself, at once humble and proud, ashamed and delighted; everything seemed to me to be like a delightful dream in which one embellishes one's image, recognizes it again as ennobled, and gladly accepts everything lovable and praiseworthy that one does and says in this elevated state; even the unmistakable cooperation of a powerful and higher being, to the extent that this cooperation endows us with qualities that we do not perhaps possess at all and dis-

covers in us others that we did not think that we had, is in its origin so gratifying that when life has bright moments of this sort, one can do nothing but accept it all as a gift from heaven.

Marianne was sure: Goethe must have felt what was happening to her, precisely because "her heart was open." She was a "puzzle" to herself in this stream of lyrical productivity; it must have been an "elevated state," even the "unmistakable cooperation of a powerful and higher being." It is clear that Marianne was not conscious in her "bright moments" of the borderline between fiction and reality, and it was only for that reason that she was able to write these poems and only for that reason that Goethe could call them "his own" because he was, in a special sense, their "originator."

The nineteenth-century scholar Hermann Grimm described a meeting with Marianne Willemer in 1850. While they were walking, a wind sprang up, and Grimm recalled Goethe's "West Wind" and quoted the lines. When Marianne asked him what had prompted him to do this, he said, "Oh, it suddenly came so vividly to mind; it is one of Goethe's most beautiful poems." Thereupon Marianne confided her life's secret to him, of course with the request that he should never speak of it. They met again, and Marianne showed Grimm the documents. He immediately recognized the importance of the discovery but he kept it to himself, even after Marianne's death on 6 December 1860 at the age of seventy-six.

It was not until nine years after her death, thirty-seven years after Goethe's death and fifty years after the appearance of the Divan, that Hermann Grimm wrote his famous study Goethe und Suleika, which appeared in 1869 in the Preussische Jahrbücher. From that time on, the authorship, at least of these three poems, has been clear.

But the question remains why Goethe himself did not say in what sense he felt himself also to be the author of these three poems.

The question really pertains to Goethe's method of literary production in the last fifteen years of his life. Did he have the feeling that he was no longer attached to the realities of life? He resumed a former practice of his: asking friends and acquaintances to describe their day's experiences and send them to him. Johann Gottfried Herder had criticized this practice as early as 1789: "Damn the god for whom everything around him has to become a question, which he uses as he pleases! Or, to put it more mildly, I distance myself from that great artist . . . who regards his friends and whatever happens to come his way merely as paper to write on."

Those immediately around him—Christiane, August, and later his secretary Caroline Ulrich—were urged to write letters, diaries, reports of their day's activities and send them to him. Goethe's diary was generally dictated to his secretaries as a draft, which they then wrote down. Caroline Ulrich is said to have written down the whole of his diary for a complete month without his having dictated anything. When his son August returned from his studies in Heidelberg, he had to wait for two weeks before his father greeted him, and first of all he had to write a report on all his experiences. Goethe's remark is significant: "If I had twelve sons, I would send each of them to a different place, so that I could learn from my own flesh and blood what things look like all over the world."

Goethe did, from time to time, use texts from third persons, but there is no parallel to the Marianne poems in the Divan. The exception is "Presence of the Beloved," in which all four stanzas open with the line "I think of you." In the first half of April 1795, Goethe was staying with the Hufeland family in Jena and heard Zelter's setting of Friederike Brun's "I think of you." "I found the melody incredibly appealing and could not resist writing a poem to it: it appears in Schiller's Musenalmanach." Goethe adopted the strophic beginning, "I think of you," but he totally changed the rest of the text.

Goethe took a broad view when adopting the observations and experiences of other people. It certainly seemed self-evident to him that Marianne's poems belonged in the Divan. And, understandably, the poetic exuberance of the poems and structure of Hafiz's "Divan" also contributed to their adoption.

In this connection, we should mention the "Confessions of a Noble Soul," which form the extensive Book 6 of Wilhelm Meisters Lehrjahre (Wilhelm Meister's apprenticeship), published without the real author's name. Unlike his silence with regard to Marianne's poems, however, Goethe does tell us who the author is in Dichtung und Wahrheit II, 8: "It is from those conversations and letters that the 'Confessions of a Noble Soul' sprang." We can be sure that texts by Susanna Katharine von Klettenberg were the basis of Goethe's "Confessions."

Eckermann, on 18 January 1825, tells us of a conversation he had with Goethe about originality. Walter Scott had used a scene from Egmont and had a right to do so. Lord Byron's metamorphosed devil was an extension of Mephistopheles, and that was right and proper. "Just as my Mephistopheles sings a song by Shakespeare, and why shouldn't he? Why should I take the trouble to write one of my own when Shakespeare's was just right and said exactly what should be said?" Here Goethe is referring to the scene "Nacht. Strasse vor Gretchens Türe" (Night. Street in front of Gretchen's door). In Mephisto's song "What are you doing / In front of my beloved's door?" Goethe introduced lines from Ophelia's song (Hamlet IV, 5) "Let in the maid, that out a maid / Never departed more." In a conversation on 14 February 1824 about the Zahme Xenien (Tame epigrams), Goethe discusses the imitation of Shakespeare with Chancellor von Müller; and on 17 December 1824 he does so once again with reference to Faust: "Does not everything that our predecessors and our contemporaries have achieved belong to [the writer] de jure? Why should he be afraid to pick flowers where he finds them? Something great comes to pass only when other people's treasures are adopted. Didn't I even adopt Job and a Shakespeare song in my depiction of Mephistopheles?"

Goethe's method of production is extremely interesting but was long neglected by Goethe scholars. Here we can only touch on the subject. In the "Historical Part" of his Farbenlehre (Theory of color) published in 1810, Goethe reflects, in a cultural context, upon the inevitability of adopting other people's material and of its use for the present.

Individuals have probably never separated themselves and individualized themselves from one another more than they do today. All people would like to constitute the universe and represent it from within themselves; but while they accept nature passionately, they are also forced to accept what has been handed down and what others have achieved. If they do not accept it consciously, they will come across it unconsciously; if they do not accept it openly and in good conscience, then they may seize it secretly and unwittingly; if they cannot recognize it thankfully, then others will be on their track; it is enough if they only know how to take directly or indirectly what is theirs and what is other people's from the hands of nature or from their predecessors, how to adapt competently what they have received, and how to mold it so that it assumes a significant individuality: this will prove to be a great advantage at any time for everyone involved. "The greatest genius would not get very far," Goethe remarked to Eckermann on 17 February 1832 (five weeks before his death), "if he drew only on himself as a source. At bottom, we are all collective beings, no matter how we like to present ourselves. For how little do we have, and how little are we, that in the purest sense we can call our own. We all have to receive and to learn, both from those who came before us and from those who are with us today. Even the greatest genius would not get far if all he wanted was to owe everything to his own inner being."

On the very same day, Goethe met with Frédéric Jean Soret. Soret was a naturalist, a theologian, and a writer from Geneva, summoned to Weimar by the Archduchess Maria Pawlowna to be a tutor to her son Karl Alexander; he was a frequent guest at Goethe's house and was very interested in his scientific writings. On this particular day they talked about Mirabeau. The French, according to Goethe, wanted to make a Hercules out of Mirabeau, but even a colossus consists of parts. What would genius be, Goethe asked, if it lacked the gift of using everything it comes into contact with? Then (Soret wrote it down in French: "Que suis-je moi-même? Qu'ai-je fait? J'ai recueilli, utilisé tout ce que j'ai entendu, observé . . . ?"): "What am I myself? What have I done? I collected, used, everything I saw, everything I heard, everything that occurred to my senses. Thousands of individuals have contributed their part to my works, fools and sages, clever people and nitwits, children, men, old and middle-aged, they all came and brought their thoughts to me, their talent, their ability, their experiences, their lives and their beings: thus I often harvested what others had sown. My life's work is that of a collective being, and this work bears the name of Goethe."[3]

---

3 Goethe in conversation with Frédéric Soret on 17 February 1832, in *Das Werk als Kolletiv Wesen mit Namen Goethe* (The work as a collective being named Goethe), translated from the French by H. H. Houben (in the 1929 edition).

Goethe, Marianne und der Gingko

Siegfried Unseld[1]

Nicht für ein großes Publikum, aber doch für den Kreis der Goethe-Kenner sind das Datum vom Freitag, dem 15. September 1815, und der Ort, die Gerbermühle bei Frankfurt, wesentlich. Viele Forscher haben ihn beschrieben und analysiert, Ernst Beutler, Konrad Burdach, Günther Debon, Ernst Grumach, Christoph Perels, Hans-J. Weitz; ich verdanke den beiden Bänden mit den Handschriften und Kommentaren zum West-östlichen Divan von Katharina Mommsen wertvolle Einsichten. An diesem 15. September 1815 waren Goethe und seine Freunde versammelt, Johann Jakob Willemer, Bankier in Frankfurt und Pächter der Gerbermühle, mit seiner Frau Marianne, und Johann Sulpiz Boisserée, der Kölner Kunstfreund. Goethe hatte ein Gingko-Blatt an Marianne Willemer geschickt und dabei die Idee erläutert: »... daß ich Eins und doppelt bin . . .«

Was ging diesem 15. September 1815 voraus, und was folgte ihm nach? Nichts weniger als die Zeit der Entstehung von Goethes bedeutendstem Gedichtwerk, dem *West-östlichen Divan*, dem einzigen, das er zu Lebzeiten als größeres lyrisches Einzelwerk selbst veröffentlicht hat.[2] Die Sammlung erschien schließlich 1819, hatte aber nach dem Erscheinen und für die nächsten 100 Jahre eine relativ geringe Resonanz. Goethe hatte ja unter den Literaten und den literarischen Meinungsmachern gerade jener Zeit mehr Feinde als Freunde. Die Schriftsteller Grabbe und Börne verrissen die Gedichte des Divan. Heinrich Heine allerdings, der gewiß nicht unkritische Dichter, erkannte ihre Bedeutung: »Den berauschendsten Lebensgenuß hat hier Goethe in Verse gebracht, und diese sind so leicht, so glücklich, so hingehaucht, so ätherisch, daß

---

1 **Siegfried Unseld** (1924-2002) was the publisher of Suhrkamp Verlag for 50 years. He wrote four previous books on Goethe, including *Goethe and His Publishers* (1996), published in English translation by the University of Chicago Press.

2 Dies ist auffallend und verdient hervorgehoben zu werden: Der West-östliche Divan ist Goethes einzige selbständige größere Lyrik-publikation. Er schrieb immer Gedichte, er veröffentlichte immer Gedichte, doch die Veröffentlichung geschah nur in Zeitschriften, in seinen Romanen, in seinen Briefen und dann im Rahmen seiner verschiedenen Werkausgaben seit 1789.

man sich wundert, wie dergleichen möglich war . . . Und die großen Goetheschen Gedanken treten dann hervor, rein und golden, wie die Sterne. Unbeschreiblich ist der Zauber dieses Buches.« Zauber auch, weil unbeabsichtigt und doch folgerichtig eine Frau, eben Marianne Willemer, in den Mittelpunkt eines Werkes treten sollte, das ebenso ein großes Werk der Weltliteratur ist wie ein Werk, das heute, bei der gegenwärtigen Auseinandersetzung westlicher Zivilisation mit dem Islam, fast aktuelle Bedeutung gewinnt.

Goethe hüllt die Entstehung dieses Gedichtwerks bewußt und spielerisch in ein Geheimnis. Er weiß zu Beginn noch nicht, wohin die Poesie ihn führen wird. Für seine Umwelt bleibt alles geheimnisvoll, so auch der zeitgeschichtliche Hintergrund, durch die letzten Napoleonischen Kriege bestimmt, der starke autobiographische Charakter und, als Zentrum des Denkens und Fühlens, die »Kleine«, die »kleine Frau«, Marianne Willemer als Muse und Initiatorin, ja als Mitautorin.

Gerade weil Goethe sein Divan-Spiel ins Geheimnis hüllt, ist von Bedeutung, daß er das wichtigste Zeugnis zur Genese des ganzen Komplexes – der sich ihm aufdrängt und der sich nun vor ein »wichtiges Geschäft«, nämlich die Neuausgabe seiner Werke, schiebt – seinem Verleger mitteilen will.

Dies in einem Brief an Verleger Cotta am 16. Mai 1815, den er dem Sekretär Kräuter diktierte, jedoch nicht abgeschickt hat: »Ich habe mich nämlich im Stillen längst mit *orientalischer Literatur* beschäftigt, und um mich inniger mit derselben bekannt zu machen, mehreres in Sinn und Art des Orients gedichtet. Meine Absicht ist dabey, auf heitere Weise den Westen und Osten, das Vergangene und Gegenwärtige, das Persische und Deutsche zu verknüpfen und beyderseitige Sitten und Denkarten übereinander greifen zu lassen.« Goethe erwähnt dankend Cottas vorjähriges Geschenk[3]. Geschenke von Verlegern an Autoren können Folgen auslösen! Am 10. Mai 1814 hatte Cotta nämlich »die Gnade«, Goethe neben verlangten Belegexemplaren von Cellini einige »Neuigkeiten« seines Verlages zu übersenden. Darunter das Buch *Der Diwan von Mohammed Schemsed-din Hafis. Aus dem Persischen zum erstenmal ganz übersetzt von Joseph von Hammer-Purgstall*, zwei Bände, Stuttgart und Tübingen 1812-1813.

---

3 Vergleiche die ausführliche Darstellung dieses Themes in meinem Buch *Goethe und seine Verleger*, inseondere das Kapital »Kleine Privatzustände an dem ungeheuren Maßstabe der Weltgeschichte gemessen: Der Divan«, S. 431-457.

Die Gnade war eine Initialzündung. Seinen Leseeindruck hält Goethe selbst fest: »Schon im vorigen Jahre waren mir die sämmtlichen Gedichte Hafis' in der von Hammer'schen Übersetzung zugekommen, und wenn ich früher den hier und da in Zeitschriften übersetzt mitgetheilten einzelnen Stücken dieses herrlichen Poeten nichts abgewinnen konnte, so wirkten sie doch jetzt *zusammen* desto lebhafter auf mich ein, und ich mußte mich dagegen productiv verhalten, weil ich sonst vor der mächtigen Erscheinung nicht hätte bestehen können. Die Einwirkung war zu lebhaft, die deutsche Übersetzung lag vor, und ich mußte also hier Veranlassung finden zu eigener Theilnahme. Alles was dem Stoff und dem Sinne nach bei mir Ähnliches verwahrt und gehegt worden, that sich hervor, und dieß mit umso mehr Heftigkeit, als ich höchst nöthig fühlte, mich aus der wirklichen Welt, die sich selbst offenbar und im Stillen bedrohte, in eine ideelle zu flüchten, an welcher vergnüglichen Theil zu nehmen meiner Lust, Fähigkeit und Willen überlassen war.«

Die Notiz wird so ausführlich wiedergegeben, weil sie einer der ganz seltenen Belege Goethes über die Auslegung des eigenen schöpferischen Prozesses ist. Gegen große Vorzüge anderer Dichter gibt es für ihn ein einziges Rettungsmittel, nämlich sich dagegen produktiv zu verhalten, es als Veranlassung eigener Teilnahme zu nehmen, das heißt, aus diesem Geiste heraus Neues zu schaffen.

Was Goethe an Hafis faszinierte, sei hier nur kurz erwähnt. Es sind Hafis' Frömmigkeit, seine Lebens- und Liebeskraft, sein Sinnengenuß, die ihn für Goethe zum »lieblichen Lebensbegleiter« werden lassen, und er bewundert die Meisterschaft seiner Poesie. Er will mit Hafis aufbrechen, fliehen. Er schreibt am 21. Juni 1814:

So, Hafis, mag Dein holder Sang,
Dein heiliges Exempel
Uns führen, bei der Gläser Klang,
Zu unsres Schöpfers Tempel.

Doch als er am 25. Juli 1814 mit Diener Stadelmann von Weimar aufbricht, geht die Reise nicht zu »unsres Schöpfers Tempel«, auch nicht so sehr, um im »reinen Osten . . . Patriarchenluft zu kosten«, es war eine Flucht aus der Weimarer Enge, aus der immer schwieriger werdenden Ehe, aus Belastungen, die die Arbeit des Ministers mit sich brachte (z. B. mußte er Stellung nehmen, ob Deserteure der Armee des Herzogs mit dem Tode bestraft werden sollten). Es war eine Flucht rückwärts und vorwärts. Zurück in die alte Heimat, vorwärts eben mit neu gefühlten Kräften, die er aus der Natur zieht: Dort gattet sich »Phöbus mit der Regenwand«, es entsteht ein »Himmelsbogen«, und als Zusicherung, als »Phänomen«, die Sicherheit: »Doch wirst Du lieben.«

Am 28. Juli 1814 kommt er in Frankfurt an. Die Reise war äußerst produktiv, da viele Gedichte entstanden. So ein Gedicht, das ursprünglich »Buch Sad, Gasele I« hieß, dann »Selbstopfer«, dann »Vollendung« und schließlich im *Divan* »Selige Sehnsucht«; ein Gedicht nicht für die Menge, die »verhöhnet«, sondern für Eingeweihte: »Sagt es niemand, nur den Weisen.« Die beiden letzten Strophen lauten:

Keine Ferne macht dich schwierig,
Kommst geflogen und gebannt,
Und zuletzt, des Lichts begierig,
Bist du Schmetterling verbrannt,

Und so lang du das nicht hast,
Dieses: Stirb und werde!
Bist du nur ein trüber Gast
Auf der dunklen Erde.

Ein großes Gedicht: »Stirb und werde«, der absolute Mittelpunkt von Goethes Gedichtwerk *West-östlicher Divan.* Goethes Vorstellung von der Seelenwanderung (»du Schmetterling«) kommt zum Ausdruck, seine Farbentheologie (die Ur-phänomene Licht und Dunkel), das Stirb und Werde, die Auferstehung der Toten, das Jesus-wort nach Markus: »Wer sein Leben findet, der wird's verlieren, und wer sein Leben verlieret um meiner willen, der wird's finden.« – Noch Brecht hat dies (auf Kosten Rilkes) in seinem Arbeitsjournal 27. 10. 1941) gelobt: ».. . wie das gelegentliche Ausgleiten ins Banale, wie in der Zeile ›dieses Stirb und Werde‹ in dem großen [sic!] Hafis-Gedicht, gerade dem Ganzen das gewisse Elementare verleiht!«

Solche Gedichte entstehen während der Reise nach Frankfurt und Wiesbaden; Ende August ist die Sammlung auf dreißig Gedichte angewachsen. Am 4. August 1814 trifft Goethe in Wiesbaden seinen Freund Willemer. Johann Jakob Willemer, 1760 geboren, 1816 nobilitiert, war Geheimer Rat und Senator, Enkel, Neffe, Vetter langer Reihen lutherischer Pastoren, Sohn und Erbe eines erfolgreichen Bankmannes, trat 1790 im Bau- und Kastenamt in die Dienste der Stadt Frankfurt. Er führte 1792 die äußerst brisanten Verhandlungen mit den Franzosen, die Frankfurt besetzt hielten und hohe Kontributionen forderten.

Willemer stellt an diesem 4. August auch flüchtig »seine kleine Gefährtin« vor, Demoiselle Jung, Marianne, die Goethes »liebe Kleine«, seine Suleika, seine Geistespartnerin im Divan werden, aber auch die Frau, für die er eine immense Leidenschaft entwickeln sollte – wie sie zu ihm. Doch es ist den beiden gelungen, den Grad ihrer intimen Beziehung ein Geheimnis bleiben zu lassen, nur sie wußten, was wirklich geschah; man darf auch nicht aus dem Dialog des »Buches Suleika« eine Liebesgeschichte dechiffrieren. Goethe gestand jedoch noch 1819: »Da fühlt ich recht, daß ich ihr, der ›geliebten Freundin‹, noch immer angehöre ... Und so fort für ewig G«. Wer war Marianne? Wer war Maria Anna Katharina Theresia Jung? Die junge Frau mit den Vornamen der Gottesmutter, von zwei Heiligen der Kirche und von Wiens größter Kaiserin: erhielt sie diese Namen als Schutz, weil sie vielleicht doch unehelich geboren war? Man weiß aus ihrer Frühzeit wenig. Demoiselle Jung, wohl am 20. November 1784 in Österreich geboren, wuchs in Wien auf. Früh ging sie zum Theater, 1793 an das Landstraßer Theater in Wien, später hatte sie ein Engagement im Preßburger Theater, dann in Baden bei Wien. Mit ihrer Mutter kam sie im November 1798 nach Frankfurt.

Seit 1798 tritt sie im Frankfurter Nationaltheater auf, in der Oper »Das unterbrochene Opferfest«, und wirkt von nun an regelmäßig in Schauspielen, Singspielen und Opern mit, nach einer Ausbildung auch als Tänzerin. Im Ballett »Die Geburt des Harlekins« sieht Clemens von Brentano sie und fühlt sich angezogen. Inzwischen ist Willemer Oberdirektor des Frankfurter Theaters geworden, und auch ihm blieb Marianne nicht verborgen. Sie ist keine schöne, aber doch eine attraktive, verführerische Erscheinung, wohlgestalt, mit glutvollen Augen, gewinnenden Locken. Willemer nimmt im Frühjahr 1800 die Schauspielerin und Tänzerin in sein bürgerlich geführtes Haus als Pflegekind auf, wo sie zusammen mit seinen Kindern, drei Töchtern aus erster Ehe und einem Sohn aus zweiter Ehe, erzogen werden soll; Mariannes Mutter erhielt 2000 Goldgulden und eine Rente auf Lebenszeit, sie war glücklich über diese Vereinbarung und kehrte nach Linz zurück. Marianne mußte sich allein in die neue Situation einfügen, und dies Lebensstück gelang ihr vollkommen.

Clemens Brentano kommt des öfteren ins Haus; er gibt Marianne Gitarrenunterricht; er verliebt sich in sie. Dann kommt es zu Spannungen mit Willemer. Als in der Familie Brentano eine Heirat von Marianne und Clemens erwogen wird, nimmt Willemers Eifersucht überhand, und er wünscht, die beiden dürften sich nicht mehr sehen. Doch noch einmal, am 10. Mai 1802, sehen sie sich. Brentano dichtet für sie das Lied »Es stehet im Abendglanze«. Danach bricht die Beziehung ab. Willemer beginnt nun selbst um Marianne zu werben. Er bemüht sich um ihre Bildung, will durch Reisen in die Schweiz und nach Italien ihren Horizont erweitern.

An dem erwähnten 4. August 1814 sieht Goethe sie zum ersten Mal. Für den fünfundsechzigjährigen Goethe war es eine »temporäre Verjüngung«, eine »wiederholte Pubertät«, wie sie der Greis im Gespräch mit Eckermann (11. 3. 1828) erläuterte: daß sie sich »bei vorzüglich begabten Menschen auch während ihres Alters immer noch ereignen« können, »während andere Leute nur einmal jung sind«.

Willemer ahnt eine aufkeimende Beziehung zwischen den beiden. Marianne selbst kann ihre Bewunderung für den Dichter nicht verbergen, und wohl auch nicht eine sich andeutende intensive Gefühlsbindung. Kurz bevor es zur zweiten Begegnung mit Goethe kommt, heiratet der vierundfünfzigjährige Willemer am 27. September 1814 die dreißigjährige Marianne. Es gab vor der Heirat ein Gespräch Willemers mit Goethe, über dessen Inhalt nichts bekannt ist außer der Vermutung, Willemer habe ihn um Rat gefragt, ob er seine Verbindung mit Marianne legitimieren solle. Man kann annehmen, Goethe habe ihm zur Heirat geraten. Wenn jemand Erfahrung über die gesellschaftliche Auswirkung unehelicher Lebensgemeinschaft hatte, zudem, wenn beide Partner die unterschiedlichsten sozialen Stellungen bekleideten, so Goethe. Er mußte freilich einen gravierenden Unterschied anerkennen. Willemer – der Goethe gegenüber bekannte: »Ich bin ohne Erziehung aufgewachsen und habe nichts gelernt« – hatte seiner Adoptivtochter und späteren Geliebten eine vorzügliche Ausbildung gegeben. Goethe, gebildet wie kein anderer, gab Christiane keine Chancen zur Bildung; er gab ihr Privilegien und half wenig, wie sie diese ausfüllen könnte. Mit gesetzten Worten wird er die Heirat begrüßen, Boisserée hat Goethes Wort in seinem Tagebuch festgehalten (3. 10. 1815): »So ist die Rettung der kleinen liebenswürdigen Frau ein großes sittliches Gut.«

18 Jahre lebte Demoiselle Jung im Hause Willemer, bis er sie heiratete; 18 Jahre war Christiane Vulpius Haushälterin, bis Goethe sie schließlich zu seiner Frau, zur Geheimrätin und späteren Staatsministerin machte. Willemers Heirat ist vollkommen überstürzt, ohne Frist und Aufgebot. Die Trauung in Frankfurt zwischen dem Lutheraner Willemer und der Katholikin Marianne nimmt der Pfarrer Kirchner von der Heilig-Geist-Kirche vor, es ist keine kirchliche, sondern eine Privattrauung. Es fehlt der Geburtsschein Mariannes, auch der Totenschein des Vaters. Die Papiere sollten aus Linz, wo Mariannes Mutter lebte, beigebracht werden, doch sie kommen nie. Deshalb wird Marianne für immer ohne das Frankfurter

Bürgerrecht bleiben müssen. Sie war und blieb in den sechzig Jahren ihres Aufenthalts in Frankfurt »Ausländerin«. Wie sollte es im »Buch der Sprüche« des Divan heißen?

Guten Ruf mußt du dir machen,
Unterscheiden wohl die Sachen;
Wer was weiter will, verdirbt.

Kurz vor der Heirat begegnet Goethe Marianne auf der Gerbermühle ein zweites Mal. Als er sie dann das dritte Mal sieht, am 12. Oktober 1814, ist sie schon Willemers, »unseres würdigen Freundes«, Frau. Goethe beeilt sich übrigens nicht, seiner Frau Christiane diese Heirat anzuzeigen. Für den 12. Oktober diktiert er dem Diener Stadelmann einen Brief an Christiane: »Abend zu Frau Geheimräthin Willemer: denn dieser unser würdiger Freund ist nunmehr in forma verheiratet. Sie ist so freundlich und gut wie vormals. Er war nicht zu Hause.« Ein dürrer Bericht, aus Gründen.

Im Oktober 1814 treffen sich Goethe und Marianne wieder in Frankfurt. Die neun Oktobertage sind ein Erlebnis für Marianne. Am 18. Oktober schauen sie gemeinsam vom Frankfurter Mühlberg aus dem Feuerwerk zum Jahrestag der Völkerschlacht bei Leipzig zu. Goethe hat diesen Tag festgehalten, für Marianne wird es ein existentiell wesentlicher Tag sein und bleiben, sie wird immer wieder auf ihn zurückkommen.

In seinem Tagebuch hält Goethe auch den letzten Tag seines Frankfurter Aufenthalts fest: »Besuche: Marianne ... abgefahren um zwei Uhr.« Am 20. Oktober tritt Goethe die Rückreise nach Weimar an. Er sollte Marianne erst wieder im Sommer 1815 sehen. Die beiden halten komplizierte, irgendwie konspirative Verbindung, über Freunde, über Töchter Willemers, über Briefe, ja selbst über Goethes verschlüsselte Briefe an Willemer. Dann mit Gedichten Goethes und mit Gedichten von Marianne. Immer bleibt es bei der Anrede »liebe Kleine«, obschon Goethe auch immer wieder im Scherz und halben Ernst vom »kleinen Blücher«, »kleinen Kritikus«, »kleinen Don Juan« spricht.

Willemer mahnt am 12. Dezember 1814 ein Lebenszeichen von Goethe an: »Meine Frau will, seitdem sie von Ihnen die Kleine genannt worden, durchaus nicht mehr wachsen, es wäre denn in Ihrem Herzen.« Goethe reagiert zwei Tage später: »Daß ich der lieben Kleinen noch ein Blättchen schuldig bin, habe nicht vergessen«, und er schickt ein Gedicht mit der Schlußstrophe:

Und so bringt vom fernen Orte
Dieses Blatt euch goldne Worte,
Wenn die Lettern schwarz gebildet;
Liebevoll der Blick vergüldet.

Diese Sommermonate 1814 waren für Goethe äußerst produktiv. Es entstanden viele Gedichte. Sie machten, so teilt er Riemer am 30. August mit, »ein kleines Ganze, das sich wohl ausdehnen kann, wenn der Humor wieder rege wird«. Er bleibt rege. Goethe findet einen neuen Titel für die bisherigen *Gedichte an Hafis*, nämlich *Deutscher Divan*. Damit hat Goethe eine tragende Konzeption gefunden. Er will noch einmal den Versuch machen – man beachte den Anspruch –, »in dieser Zeit unsere kleinen Privatzustände an dem ungeheuren Maßstab der Weltgeschichte zu messen«. Sein persönliches Erleben (er beschreibt es mit »Sorge, Furcht, Angst, Schrecken und Leiden«) sieht er vor dem Hintergrund der politischen Ereignisse dieser Jahre, in denen eine Epoche endete und eine neue begann, in der Napoleon aufstieg und fiel, in der das Heilige Römische Reich unterging und der Versuch einer neuen Friedensordnung unternommen wurde. So werden ihm die Gedichte des *Divan* in diesem Stadium zum »Vehikel seines politischen Glaubensbekenntnisses«. Wie sehr irren jene, die Goethe in den elfenbeinernen Turm versetzen, ihn einen apolitischen Menschen nennen, der vor der Wirklichkeit flieht.

Im Mai 1815 ordnet Goethe die bisher entstandenen 100 Gedichte. Er glaubt, der *Divan* sei abgeschlossen. Aber es fehlten die von ihm beabsichtigten »Noten und Abhandlungen« zum besseren Verständnis:

Wer das Dichten will verstehen
Muß in's Land der Dichtung gehen;
Wer den Dichter will verstehen
Muß in Dichters Lande gehen.

Am 24. Mai 1815 bricht Goethe von Weimar nach Wiesbaden auf, er reist zwar über Frankfurt, sieht aber die Willemers nicht und hat auch keine Eile, sie wiederzusehen. Unterwegs und in Wiesbaden arbeitet er am *Divan* weiter; es entstehen Gedichte, die er später dem geplanten »Buch der Liebe« und dem »Buch Suleika« zuordnet, darunter, am 24. Mai 1815 entstanden, die Verse:

Da du nun Suleika heißest
Sollt ich auch benamset seyn.
Wenn du deinen Geliebten preisest,
Hatem! das soll der Name seyn.

Damit hat Goethe Suleika (und sich) »benamst«, aber er meinte hier nicht (noch nicht) Marianne (wie einer der ersten Interpreten, Hans Pyritz, 1941 festzustellen glaubte). Marianne war und blieb damals seine »liebe Kleine«, die stets mit Grüßen bedacht wurde.[4]

Am 21. Juni wird in Wiesbaden – so Goethe in seinen *Tag- und Jahres-Heften* – die Schlacht von Waterloo (18. 6. 1815) »zu großem Schrecken als verloren gemeldet, sodann zu überraschender, ja betäubender Freude, als gewonnen angekündigt«.

Dies ist der Anfang jener sechs Wochen, die Goethe später als »allerschönste Zeit« bezeichnen sollte. Sie beginnt auf der Gerbermühle, einem unmittelbar im Südosten vor Frankfurt gelegenen ländlichen Wohnsitz, welchen Willemer auf Lebenszeit gepachtet hatte. Für Goethes »Betrachtungen« war es der »angenehmste Ort«. Marianne verwöhnt ihn. Sie schildert das tägliche Ritual: Morgens war Goethe allein, zu Mittag erschien er im Frack, nachmittags liebte er Spaziergänge; abends war er am liebenswürdigsten, wenn er in seinem weißen Flanellrock erschien und Gedichte vorlas, meist Gedichte aus dem Divan-Bereich; beim Essen sei er »einfach« gewesen, mit Vorlieben für Artischocken. Er führte einen Wein bei sich, von dem er um zehn Uhr, zum zweiten Frühstück, aus einem selbst mitgebrachten silbernen Becher trank. Später faßt Marianne ihre Erinnerung an diese Tage zusammen (an Herman Grimm, 12. 5. 1853): »Goethe! ja wer ihn kannte! Wärest du mir gegenüber, ich könnte dir wohl von ihm erzählen, was nicht alle wissen; wenn sich die Strahlen seines Geistes in seinem Herzen conzentrierten, das war eine Beleuchtung, die einen eigenen Blick verlangte, es war wie Mondlicht und Sonnenlicht, eines nach dem anderen, oder auch wohl zugleich, und daraus erklärte sich auch jenes Wundervolle seines Wesens, sein gewahr werden, sich klar machen und für andre zur wahren aber verklärten Erscheinung bringen. Genug!«

Als Goethe Marianne am 12. August trifft, hat er für sie den *Diwan* des persischen Dichters Hafis im Gepäck – es soll wieder ein folgenreiches Geschenk werden. Der Abend ist für Goethe besonders beglückend. Marianne greift zur Gitarre, dem uns noch erhaltenen Instrument, statt mit den gewöhnlichen sechs mit acht Saiten bespannt und zuvor auf der italienischen Reise in Neapel gekauft. Was sie zu singen liebte, das überliefert uns wieder Boisserées Tagebuch: »Reich mir die Hand mein Leben«, »Der Gott und die Bajadere«, »Kennst du das Land«, »O gib

---

4 Gäbe es eine Verfilmung dieser Beziehung, so hätte der Darsteller Goethes wie Humphrey Bogart in »Casablanca« zu sprechen: »Ich schau dir in die Augen, Kleines«

vom weichen Pfühle«, dazu österreichische Volkslieder – war sie doch selbst allen Vermutungen nach ein Wiener Kind und selber »ein kleiner Don Juan«. Die hohe Zeit des *West-östlichen Divans*, das Hatem- und Suleika-Spiel, hat schon begonnen. Goethe trägt ins Tagebuch für diesen Tag geheimnisvoll und beziehungsreich ein: »Divan. Anfang – Ende.« Was mag er damit gemeint haben? Ist »Anfang und Ende« dieser wichtige, wichtigste Teil des *Divan*, der Wechselgesang Hatem – Suleika? EinWechselgesang, der immer mehr zum poetischen Gespräch Goethe – Marianne wird: Sie, Marianne, die »Du jetzt mich liebst«, soll Suleika sein und »sollst mir ewig Suleika heißen«.

Goethe wohnt vom 8. Bis 15. September in Willemers Stadthaus »Zum Roten Männchen«. Die Abende verbringt er meistens auf der Gerbermühle. Er ist viel zusammen mit seinem Freund Sulpiz Boisserée, mit dem er Kunstausstellungen besucht und Fahrten nach Mainz unternimmt. Aus dieser Zeit datiert Goethes Bemerkung über die Vaterstadt: »Frankfurt stickt voller Merkwürdigkeiten.«

Die Gespräche bis zum Abend des 15. September hat Boisserée sorgfältig aufgezeichnet. Die Themen: Betrachtungen der römischen Altertümer. Haben wir schon einmal gelebt? Gibt es die Seelenwanderung? Pantheismus, Monotheismus, Expansion und Konzentration. Es geht um Goethes Lehre von der Polarität allen Seins, von Systole und Diastole.

Am Freitag, dem 15. September 1815, fährt Goethe in Boisserées Begleitung von Willemers Stadthaus wieder zur Gerbermühle. Wieder sprechen sie über Kunst. Boisserée, der Katholik, glaubt an den christlichen Gehalt der Kunst, Goethe an die ästhetische Substanz. Boisserée findet das Bild des gotischen Spitzbogens, bei dem sich zwei Schenkel in einem Punkt treffen.

Wird Goethe hier wieder in seiner Auffassung des Einen und Doppelten bestärkt?

Den Abend des 15. September auf der Gerbermühle beschreibt Boisserée im Tagebuch (desselben Datums) den »heiteren Abend«: »Wir saßen in der schönen, warmen Abendluft auf dem Balkon. Marianne singt mit besonderem Affekt und Rührung.« Wir kennen den Vorgang, der den ganzen Abend bestimmt: Goethe hatte Marianne ein Gingko-Blatt geschickt, das er am Nachmittag von einem Gingko-Baum (höchstwahrscheinlich im Brentanopark) gepflückt hatte, und er hatte Zeilen dazu geschrieben, einen – wie Boisserée meinte – »Vers«, in dem es hieß: »... daß ich Eins und doppelt bin«. Auf diesen »Vers« ist man am Abend immer wieder zurückgekommen, denn, so Boisserée: »G. hatte der Wilmer ein Blatt des Ginkho biloba als Sinnbild der Freundschaft geschickt aus der Stadt. Man weiß nicht ob es eins, das sich in 2 teilt, oder zwei die sich in eins verbinden. So war der Inhalt des Verses.« Mit »Vers«, so vermuten auch Katharina Mommsen und Hans-J. Weitz, hat Goethe wohl die zweite Strophe des späteren Gedichts »Gingo biloba« gemeint. Jedenfalls kam die Gesellschaft an diesem Abend des 15. September immer wieder auf die Formulierung zurück: »... daß ich Eins und doppelt bin.«

Was aber an diesem Abend nur Goethe und Marianne wußten, war noch ein anderes. Am 15. September, also drei Tage vor diesem Abend, erhielt Marianne ein Gedicht von Goethe, das erste an sie direkt gerichtete Gedicht. Es ist mit »Hatem« überschrieben, und Goethe ist gemeint:

Hatem

Nicht Gelegenheit macht Diebe,
Sie ist selbst der größte Dieb,
Denn sie stahl den Rest der Liebe
Die mir noch im Herzen blieb.

Dir hat sie ihn übergeben
Meines Lebens Vollgewinn,
Daß ich nun, verarmt, mein Leben
Nur von dir gewärtig bin.

Doch ich fühle schon Erbarmen
Im Carfunkel deines Blicks
Und erfreu' in deinen Armen
Mich erneuerten Geschicks.

Goethe, der Sechsundsechzigjährige, fühlt sich in die Rolle des jugendlichen Sängers Hatem ein, er spürt »Frühlingsrausch und Sommerbrand«. Marianne ist seine Suleika, die Suleika des von ihm dann später geschaffenen »Buch Suleika«: »Sollst mir ewig Suleika heißen.«

Freude des Daseyns ist groß,
Größer die Freud' am Daseyn,
Wenn du Suleika
Mich überschwänglich beglückst ...

Goethes Gedicht ist eine einzige eindeutige Erklärung. Von des »Lebens Vollgewinn« ist die Rede, davon, daß ich »nur von dir gewärtig bin« und daß er sich »erneuerten Geschicks« erfreut. Goethe, der Erfahrene, geht hier aus sich heraus, und er wird erahnen, was in Marianne vorgeht, in dieser Frau, die ein Leben lang in ihren Gefühlen unerfüllt geblieben ist und nun in dem von ihr so geliebten Mann eine Erfüllung sieht. Aber Goethe ist nicht nur der Liebende, er ist der Dichter, der schafft, schreibt, der schöpferisch ist, der eben eins und doppelt ist. Die dichterische Form ist immer schon Distanz zum konkreten Erleben. Und: Er fühlt »Erbarmen« im Karfunkel ihres Blicks. Wir Heutigen müssen erkennen, daß Goethe immer der großartige Regisseur seines eigenen Lebenskunstwerks war, daß er hier zwar den großen Gewinn einer schöpferischen Muse erkannte, gleichzeitig aber auch das für ihn notwendige Scheitern einer Beziehung, der Liebe zwischen zwei anderweitig gebundenen Menschen mitkalkulierte, ja mit-inszenierte.

Marianne, und dies ist das Wunder ihrer Existenz, antwortet vier Tage später mit einem Gedicht, das die entgegengebrachte Liebe ebenso deutlich erwidert, das poetische Kraft aufweist und das dem Empfänger alle Ehre macht. Und mit dem sie der deutschen Sprache, im betonten Anfang, ein eher ungewöhnliches Wort wiedergibt: »hochbeglückt«. Hatte sie dieses Epitheton »Wilhelm Meisters theatralischer Sendung« entnommen, dort vom Harfner gesungen als Antwort auf Wilhelms Aufforderung, ihm zu vertrauen?

Der poetische Wechselgesang zwischen Marianne und Goethe beginnt. Am 16. September, einem Samstag, schreibt Marianne für Goethe:

Suleika

Hochbeglückt in deiner Liebe
Schelt ich nicht Gelegenheit,
Ward sie auch an dir zum Diebe
Wie mich solch ein Raub erfreut!

Und wozu denn auch berauben?
Gieb dich mir aus freyer Wahl,
Gar zu gerne möchte ich glauben –
Ja! Ich bin's die dich bestahl.

Was so willig du gegeben
Bringt dir herrlichen Gewinn,
Meine Ruh, mein reiches Leben
Geb' ich freudig, nimm es hin.

Scherze nicht! Nichts von Verarmen!
Macht uns nicht die Liebe reich?
Halt ich dich in meinen Armen,
Jedem Glück ist meines gleich.

Der Meister nimmt das Zeugnis der Huldigung entgegen, er korrigiert den Text leicht, schreibt ihn ab und legt ihn zu den anderen Manuskripten. Auf den 17. September datiert sind die Handschriften des später ins Buch »Suleika« aufgenommenen Dialoges, der ebenfalls von Marianne ausgeht: »Als ich auf dem Euphrat schiffte . . .« und die Antwort Hatems: »Dies zu deuten bin erbötig!«

Goethe antwortet und handelt als Autor. Aber er kann, spätestens nach dem Gedicht »Hochbeglückt in deiner Liebe«, nicht übersehen, was er bei Marianne angerichtet hat. Sie liebt ihn mit allen Fasern ihres Wesens. So beginnt sein »Duo-drama«, und Goethe reagiert, wie er in solchen für ihn ausweglosen Situationen immer reagiert hat: mit einer Flucht. Am 18. September 1815 verläßt Goethe die Gerbermühle, verläßt er Frankfurt. Er eilt nach Heidelberg, um sich dort mit gelehrten Orientalisten, den »Wissenden«, zu besprechen. Er teilt Willemers mit, daß sein Rückweg nicht über Frankfurt führe. Aber was er nicht wissen kann: daß Willemers unerwartet und unangemeldet am 23. September in Heidelberg auftauchen. Marianne hat es nicht ausgehalten, ihn nicht mehr zu sehen. Goethe führt Marianne in den Schloßgarten und zeigt ihr den dortigen Gingko-Baum. Nach der Zusendung des Blattes und dem Abend in der Gerbermühle ist es nun das dritte Mal, daß Goethe sie auf den Gingko aufmerksam macht und ihr den »geheimen Sinn« erklärt: »Ist es eins, das sich in zwei teilt, oder zwei, die sich in eins verbinden?«

Am Abschiedstag, am 26. September, spazieren Willemers und Goethe durch den Heidelberger Park. Er nimmt Marianne zur Seite und führt sie an den Brunnen. Dann schreibt er in arabischen Schriftzeichen (die er am Tage vorher bei einem »Wissenden«, dem Orientalisten Heinrich Eberhard Gottlob Paulus, gelernt hat) den Namen Suleika in den Sand. Die Willemers verlassen Heidelberg, immer noch in der Hoffnung, Goethe wiederzusehen. Er aber weiß es anders. Er weiß, daß ein Wiedersehen nicht sein darf. Im Tagebuch vom 25. September lesen wir: »Abend-

Music. Gespräch. Abschied.« Am 26. September: »Abreise der Freunde. Divan. Blieb zu Hause.« Marianne sollte Goethe nie wiedersehen. Er selber ist bewegt. Sein Herz meldet sich mit Klopfen und Pochen. In seiner Verzweiflung stürzt er sich in persische Studien, besucht Professor Creuzer, spricht mit ihm über die Symbolträchtigkeit und Vieldeutigkeit der antiken Mythen. Jede Gestalt, so Creuzer, sei doppeldeutig. Goethe sagte ihm: »Also ungefähr wie dieses Blatt, eins und doppelt.«

Dann in der Stimmung des endgültigen Abschieds, der Trennung von einer Liebe, die er opfert, auch um sein Werk, seine »Lieder« fortführen zu können, schreibt Goethe das Gedicht mit dem späteren Titel »Gingo biloba«. Am 27. September schickt er es nach Frankfurt. Er richtet die Sendung jedoch nicht direkt an Marianne, obschon sie als einzige Empfängerin gelten muß, sondern an ihre Freundin und Willemers Tochter Rosine Städel. Ihr erläutert er, daß er zu der prosaischen Auslegung, die das »bekannte, wunderliche Blatt« an jenem Abend in der Gerbermühle erfahren hat, nun eine »rhythmische Übersetzung«, sprich ein Gedicht, geschrieben habe.

Es gibt drei Fassungen dieses Gedichts, die textlich freilich nur geringfügig voneinander abweichen, weil aber jede noch so geringe Abweichung zur Deutung des Gedichts beitragen kann, seien hier alle Fassungen zitiert. I. Fassung: jenes Gedicht, das Goethe am 27. September an Rosine Städel für Marianne schickt:

> *Dieses Baums Blat, der, von Osten,*
> *Meinem Garten anvertraut,*
> *Giebt geheimen Sinn zu kosten,*
> *Wie's den Wissenden erbaut.*
> *Ist es Ein lebendig Wesen?*
> *Das sich in sich selbst getrennt;*
> *Sind es Zwey? die sich erlesen,*
> *Daß man sie als Eines kennt.*
> *Solche Frage zu erwiedern*
> *Fand ich wohl den rechten Sinn;*
> *Fühlst du nicht an meinen Liedern,*
> *Daß ich Eins und doppelt bin?*

II. Fassung: Wie Günther Debon nachwies, ist die bekannte, auch von Katharina Mommsen in ihrer Sammlung der Niederschriften des *Divan* wiedergegebene Handschrift eine Beilage zu einem Brief Goethes an den Großherzog Carl August vom 10. März 1820: »Ew. Königliche Hoheit erhalten hiebey die angekündigte Wiener Sendung: [...] 2) Über den Gingko, von Freyherrn von Jacquin.«

Goethe folgt der naturwissenschaftlichen Übung, den von Linné nun einmal eingeführten Namen zu übernehmen. Das von Goethe hier angegebene Datum »d. 15. S. 1815« ist jedoch nicht das Entstehungsdatum des Gedichts, sondern die Erinnerung an den Abend auf der Gerbermühle, die für Goethe die Keimzelle des Gedichts ist.

> *Ginkgo biloba.*
>
> *Dieses Baums Blatt, der von Osten*
> *Meinem Garten anvertraut,*
> *Giebt geheimen Sinn zu kosten*
> *Wie's den Wissenden erbaut.*
>
> *Ist es Ein lebendig Wesen,*
> *Das sich in sich selbst getrennt,*
> *Sind es zwey die sich erlesen,*
> *Daß man sie als Eines kennt.*
>
> *Solche Frage zu erwiedern*
> *Fand ich wohl den rechten Sinn,*
> *Fühlst du nicht an meinen Liedern*
> *Daß ich Eins und doppelt bin.*

III. Fassung: Der Erstdruck des Gedichts in der Buchausgabe des *West-östlichen Divan* von 1819:

> *Gingo biloba.*
>
> *Dieses Baum's Blatt, der von Osten*
> *Meinem Garten anvertraut,*
> *Giebt geheimen Sinn zu kosten,*
> *Wie's den Wissenden erbaut.*
>
> *Ist es Ein lebendig Wesen?*
> *Das sich in sich selbst getrennt,*
> *Sind es zwey? die sich erlesen,*
> *Daß man sie als eines kennt.*

Solche Frage zu erwiedern
Fand ich wohl den rechten Sinn;
Fühlst du nicht an meinen Liedern
Daß ich Eins und doppelt bin?

Im Brief an Rosine Städel spielt Goethe sein Divan-Spiel: »Hiermit nun, liebe Rosette, überliefre ich Ihnen [das Gedicht] mit den sämtlichen Geheimnissen der neuern Philologie, auch meine eignen, zu beliebigem Privatgebrauch.« Dieser Hinweis erlaubt im Hinblick auf die Entstehung, auf die Gespräche in der Gerbermühle, auf Heidelberg, auf die Stellung des Gedichts im »Buch Suleika« jedenfalls eine doppelte Auslegung, eine erotische wie eine poetisch-hermeneutische, sein Werk, sein Dichten im ganzen betreffend.

Das Gedicht, in drei Strophen zu jeweils vier Versen in vierhebigen Trochäen, thematisiert den Auftrag des Schriftstellers. Die erste Strophe fragt nach dem »geheimen Sinn« dieses »Baum's Blatt«, eine auffallende, deiktische Alliteration. Die zweite Strophe formuliert das Paradox von Einheit und Zweiheit als Rätsel. In der dritten Strophe dann – als Antwort auf den »geheimen Sinn« – der »rechte Sinn«, die Auflösung des Rätsels.

Doch in allen Stadien verwebt sich Lebensgeschichtliches. Zwei Liebende werden im Akt des Liebens eins, und doch weiß Hatem, weiß Goethe, daß Zweisamkeit immer auch Einsamkeit bedingt. So wie das Blatt, das sich nach Goethe teilen möchte, trennt, um sich doch im Doppel als Ganzes zu verstehen. Zwei als eines? »Solche Frage« zu erwidern ist der Sinn des Gedichts. Kein Zufall, daß hier »bin« und »Sinn« als Reimpaar korrespondieren. Und Hatems – Goethes – Antwort kommt sogleich. Mit dem einfachen Versschema, dem Trochäus (griech. trochaios = Läufer), mit einfachen Kreuzreimen, mit reflexiven, eigentlich trockenen Fügungen, die kaum mit Adjektiven geschmückt sind und denen Goethes sonstige Farbigkeit fehlt, stürzt das Gedicht auf die letzte Zeile: Fühlst du, Leser, fühlst du, Marianne, nicht an dem, was ich schreibe, »daß ich Eins und doppelt bin?«

Er ist der Liebende und der Geliebte, aber gleichzeitig ist er der Dichter, der in seinen Liedern, in seinen Gedichten, in seinen Werken existent ist. – Ist er nur in seinen Liedern existent? Nicht als Liebender und Geliebter? Ist er so »Eins und doppelt«? Das Ich, das Subjekt, und das Er, das Objekt seines Werks.

Auch sie ist Liebende und Geliebte. Doch während Goethe als Stratege seines Lebenskunstwerks in Extremsituationen das Prinzip Distanz kennt, vor Bindungen zurückschreckt, im wahrsten Sinne weg-geht, entsagt, doch immer zu neuem Erleben bereit ist, so wenn er bei der Rückfahrt am 7. Oktober in Hardheim beim Mittagessen ein »junges, frisches Mädchen« sieht und küßt – ist Marianne verzweifelt, sie stürzt in Depressionen und Krankheiten. Sie hat den Anteil an Phantasie, den Goethe einbrachte, nicht erkannt und deshalb die Grenze zwischen Fiktion und Wirklichkeit nicht respektieren können. Er hatte sie als Suleika zum Stern der Sterne erhoben – so mußte ihr Fall tief sein, als Goethe sich aus ihrem Leben entwand.

Wir haben einen wesentlichen Aspekt außer acht gelassen. Als Marianne nach Heidelberg kam und dort Goethe überraschte, übergab sie ihm ein Gedicht, das sie auf der Fahrt nach Heidelberg geschrieben hatte: »Was bedeutet die Bewegung? Bringt der Ost mir frohe Kunde?«

Suleika:

Was bedeutet die Bewegung?
Bringt der Ost mir frohe Kunde?
Seiner Schwingen frische Regung
Kühlt des Herzens tiefe Wunde.

Kosend spielt er mit dem Staube,
Jagt ihn auf in leichten Wölkchen,
Treibt zur sichern Rebenlaube
Der Insecten frohes Völkchen.

Lindert sanft der Sonne Glühen,
Kühlt auch mir die heißen Wangen,
Küßt die Reben noch im Fliehen,
Die auf Feld und Hügel prangen.

Und mir bringt sein leises Flüstern
Von dem Freunde tausend Grüße;
Eh noch diese Hügel düstern
Grüßen mich wohl tausend Küsse.

Und so kannst du weiter ziehen!
Diene Freunden und Betrübten.
Dort wo hohe Mauern glühen
Find' ich bald den Vielgeliebten.

Ach! die wahre Herzenskunde,
Liebeshauch, erfrischtes Leben
Wird mir nur aus seinem Munde,
Kann mir nur sein Athem geben.

Auf die »frohe Kunde«, also auf das ›Ostwind‹- Gedicht, auf dem Wege nach Heidelberg entstanden, folgt nur einige Tage später ein Lied an den ›Westwind‹, Heidelberg verlassend, das Leiden an der Trennung:

Suleika:

Ach! um deine feuchten Schwingen,
West, wie sehr ich dich beneide:
Denn du kannst ihm Kunde bringen
Was ich in der Trennung leide.

Die Bewegung deiner Flügel
Weckt im Busen stilles Sehnen,
Blumen, Augen, Wald und Hügel
Stehn bey deinem Hauch in Thränen.

Doch dein mildes sanftes Wehen
Kühlt die wunden Augenlieder;
Ach für Leid müßt' ich vergehen,
Hofft' ich nicht zu sehn ihn wieder.

Eile denn zu meinem Lieben,
Spreche sanft zu seinem Herzen;
Doch vermeid' ihn zu betrüben
Und verbirg ihm meine Schmerzen.

Sag ihm, aber sag's bescheiden:
Seine Liebe sey mein Leben,
Freudiges Gefühl von beyden
Wird mir seine Nähe geben.

Es sind zwei wunderbare Gedichte, beide aus dem Geiste der Dichtung Goethes und auch aus dem Geist von Hafis (in den sich Marianne, o Wunder, so rasch und tief eingefühlt hatte). Es sind Gedichte, die denen Goethes ebenbürtig sind und sie vielleicht in diesem Fall an Hingabe und Wärme übertreffen.

Es ist erstaunlich, wie gut sie jene Kunst erlernte, die Goethe in den *Noten und Abhandlungen* unter der Rubrik »Chiffer« beschrieben hat: »Wenn nämlich zwei Personen, die ein Buch verabreden und, indem sie Seiten- und Zeilenzahl zu einem Briefe verbinden, gewiß sind, daß der Empfänger mit geringem Bemühen den Sinn zusammenfinden werde.« In diesen Chiffer-Gedichten von Marianne sind einzelne Striche und Zeilen aus den Gedichten von Hafis und Goethe so kunstvoll komponiert, daß über die Bekundung von Liebe über ein sinnvolles poetisches Spiel hinaus »Lieder vom schönsten Ausdruck« entstanden.

Goethe, als er die Tiefe des Gefühls und die Kunst der Poesie wahrgenommen hatte, war höchst erregt. Er reagierte »doppelt«. Einmal schrieb er selbst in den Heidelberger Tagen Gedichte, die zu seinen schönsten zählen: »Wiederfinden«, weil Goethe Marianne unerwartet wiedergefunden hatte; wieder das Gingko- biloba-Thema von der Einheit in der Zweiheit, vom Auseinandergerissensein und Wiederfinden, doch wird es auf Liebe wie auf die ganze Welt bezogen; die Weltschöpfung entsteht aus der Trennung von Licht und Dunkel. Dann singt Hatem im Gedicht: »Locken! haltet mich gefangen« und: »Rast ein Ätna dir hervor«. In diesem Gedicht erlaubt er, der sonst alles in Geheimnis hüllt, eine Fast-Enthüllung:

> *Du beschämst wie Morgenröthe*
> *Jener Gipfel ernste Wand,*
> *Und noch einmal fühlet . . .*

Jetzt müßte gemäß dem Reim »Morgenröte« nach »fühlet« der Name »Goethe« stehen, doch es heißt reimlos, wenn auch bezeichnend:

> *. . . fühlet Hatem*
> *Frühlingshauch und Sommerbrand.*

Goethe klebt die Reinschrift der Gedichte »Ostwind« und »Westwind« in sein Manuskriptoriginal des *Divan* ein; dort liegt schon das Gedicht »Hochbeglückt in deiner Liebe«.

Goethe kam nie mehr in die Landschaft seiner Kindheit. Auf seiner Fahrt an den Rhein im Juli 1816 wollte er seine Vaterstadt ausdrücklich nicht besuchen. (»Meinen Weg werde über Würzburg nehmen, um das uneinige Frankfurt in diesem Augenblick nicht zu berühren.«) Aber die Achse seines Wagens brach, und er blieb in Thüringen.

Der *Divan* erschien 1819. Er war, wie erwähnt, bei Erscheinen nicht unumstritten; noch hundert Jahre später konnte man in deutschen Buchhandlungen Exemplare der ersten Auflage vorfinden. Doch dann setzte sich die Bedeutung dieses großen lyrischen Werkes durch. Felix Mendelssohn-Bartholdy, Franz Schubert und Robert Schumann haben die Gedichte vertont, sie sind zum Liedschatz deutscher Lyrik geworden.

Marianne hielt lose briefliche Verbindung mit Goethe. Am 25. August 1824 schickt sie ihm »zum Fest Ihrer Geburt« von der Gerbermühle aus einen Brief: »Der Main ist dunkelblau, die Wolken beinahe grün, und der Berg ist violett, ganz so wie damals; aber einer fehlt, der es betrachtet und deutet und andere dadurch beglückt ... Gedenken Sie meiner und in Liebe, daß ich Ihrer gedenke, möge Nachstehendes beweisen.« In dem Brief lag ein Gedicht:

Das Heidelberger Schloß, den 28. Juli abends 7 Uhr

Euch grüß ich weite, lichtumfloßne Räume,
Dich alten reichbekränzten Fürstenbau,
Euch grüß ich hohe, dichtumlaubte Bäume,
Und über euch des Himmels tiefes Blau.

Wohin den Blick das Auge forschend wendet
In diesem blütenreichen Friedensraum,
Wird mir ein leiser Liebesgruß gesendet
Aus meines Lebens freudevollstem Traum.

An der Terrasse hohem Berggeländer
War eine Zeit sein Kommen und sein Gehn,
Die Zeichen, treuer Neigung Unterpfänder,
Sie sucht ich, und ich kann sie nicht erspähn.

Dort jenes Baumsblatt, das aus fernem Osten
Dem westöstlichen Garten anvertraut,
Gibt mir geheimnisvollen Sinn zu kosten
Woran sich fromm die Liebende erbaut.

Durch jene Halle trat der hohe Norden
 Bedrohlich unserm friedlichen Geschick;
Die rauhe Nähe kriegerischer Horden
Betrog uns um den flüchtgen Augenblick.

Dem kühlen Brunnen, wo die klare Quelle
Um grünbekränzte Marmorstufen rauscht,
Entquillt nicht leiser, rascher, Well auf Welle,
Als Blick um Blick, und Wort um Wort sich tauscht.

O! schließt euch nun ihr müden Augenlider.
Im Dämmerlichte jener schönen Zeit
Umtönen mich des Freundes hohe Lieder,
Zur Gegenwart wird die Vergangenheit.

Aus Sonnenstrahlen webt ihr Abendlüfte
Ein goldnes Netz um diesen Zauberort,
Berauscht mich, nehmt mich hin ihr Blumendüfte,
Gebannt durch eure Macht kann ich nicht fort.

Schließt euch um mich ihr unsichtbaren Schranken
Im Zauberkreis der magisch mich umgibt,
Versenkt euch willig Sinne und Gedanken,
Hier war ich glücklich, liebend und geliebt.

Man hört die Nähe zum Gingo-Gedicht, zu seinem Schöpfer, und fühlt das dem Fünfundsiebzigjährigen entschwundene Glück: »Hier war ich glücklich, liebend und geliebt.« Ernst Beutler, einer der großen Kenner Goethes, schrieb: »Diese drei Gedichte Mariannens, das auf Heidelberg und die beiden an den Wind als Liebesboten, sind die schönsten Dichtungen, die je eine deutsche Frau geschaffen hat.« Das ist ein zu hohes Lob, und man kann durchaus auch Unterschiede zwischen den zwei Ost-West-Gedichten und diesem letzten Gedicht auf Heidelberg finden. Fraglos sind es bedeutende Gedichte, die Frau, die sie schrieb, eine Dichterin.

Der im *Divan* bekundete Wechselgesang ist einzigartig in der Geschichte der Literatur. Es gibt zwar die großen (literarischen) Geliebten und Liebenden, Beatrice, Laura, Diotima; es gibt die poetischen Wechselgesänge, wie z. B. Ausonius und Paulinus von Nola – doch kaum Beispiele männlich-weiblicher gemeinsamer Produktion auf höchstem poetischem Niveau.

Am 10. Februar 1832 bereitete Goethe die Rücksendung der von ihm gesammelten Briefe vor:
> Indem ich die mir gegönnte Zeit ernstlich anwende, die grenzenlosen Papiere, die sich um mich versammelt

haben, [um sie] zu sichten und darüber zu bestimmen: so leuchten mir besonders gewisse Blätter entgegen, die auf die schönsten Tage meines Lebens hindeuten; dergleichen sind manche von jeher abgesondert, nunmehr aber eingepackt und versiegelt. Ein solches Paket liegt nun mit Ihrer Adresse vor mir, und ich möcht es Ihnen gleich jetzt, allen Zufälligkeiten vorzubeugen, zusenden; nur würde mir das einzige Versprechen ausbitten, daß Sie es uneröffnet bei sich, bis zu unbestimmter Stunde, liegen lassen. Dergleichen Blätter geben uns das frohe Gefühl, daß wir gelebt haben; dies sind die schönsten Dokumente, auf denen man ruhen darf.

Am 29. Februar 1832 schickte Goethe dieses schon 1831 entstandene Gedicht zusammen mit dem versiegelten Paket ihrer Briefe ab:

Frau Geheimräthin von Willemer Gnaden.
Frankfurt am Mayn.

Vor die Augen meiner Lieben,
Zu den Fingern die's geschrieben, –
Einst, mit heißestem Verlangen
So erwartet, wie empfangen –
Zu der Brust der sie entquollen,
Diese Blätter wandern sollen;
Immer liebevoll bereit,
Zeugen allerschönster Zeit.

Weimar d. 3. März 1831.   J W v Goethe

Dies der Bogen von 1814 und dem Suleika-Jahr 1815 bis zum Todesjahr Goethes, wo er die Bekundung »allerschönster Zeit« ausspricht. Ob er wohl bei der Adressierung »Zu den Fingern die's geschrieben« neben den Briefen auch an die Gedichte des *Divan* gedacht hat?

Im Herbst 1860 ein letztes Echo. Die Sechsundsiebzigjährige möchte nochmals von der Gerbermühle nach Heidelberg, und sie fährt auch dorthin, steht im Schloßgarten am Brunnen, wo Goethe ihren Namen eingeritzt hat. Sie erzählt:»Hier hat er mich geküßt . . . Hier schrieb er mit seinem Stock einen Vers in den Sand.« Und von dem Gingko-Baum berichtet sie:»Dies ist der Baum, von welchem er mir damals [auf die Gerbermühle] ein Blatt brachte.« Sie offenbart ihrer Begleiterin, was damals außer Boisserée und Herman Grimm niemand wissen konnte, daß sie die Suleika des *Divan* sei, »aber davon weiß die Welt nichts, und es ist ja auch nicht nötig, daß es alle Leute erfahren«.

Goethes Divan erschien im Herbst 1819: *West-oestlicher Divan. Von Goethe. Stuttgard in der Cottaischen Buchhandlung 1819.* Mit Titelkupfer und gestochenem Titelblatt (nach Goethes Entwürfen). Der Band enthält die drei nahezu unveränderten Gedichte Mariannes »Hochbeglückt in deiner Liebe«, »Was bedeutet die Bewegung?«, »Ach! Um deine feuchten Schwingen«; auch das Gedicht, das, wie Marianne sagte, auf »ihr Gewissen« ging: »Sag du hast wohl viel gedichtet?« Und vermutlich hat sie noch andere Gedichte oder Textstellen angeregt.

Es gibt von Goethe keine Begründung, warum er diese Gedichte in sein Buch aufnahm und warum er die Verfasserschaft von Marianne Willemer nicht erwähnte. Selbstverständlich konnte er annehmen, daß ein kleiner Freundeskreis seine Beziehung zu Marianne und damit den auto-biographischen Hintergrund der Fiktion des Wechselgesanges Suleika/Hatem kannte. Aber niemand außer den beiden selbst wußte von der wörtlichen Übernahme der Gedichte. Dies Geheimnis wurde bewahrt bis 1869.

Goethe schickte am 22. August 1819 ein Aushängeexemplar des *Divan* an Willemer, »komplette Exemplare erhalt ich so spät, daß ich sie nicht einmal kann einbinden lassen«. Als im November die gebundenen Exemplare vorliegen, sandte Goethe eines an Marianne und trug ihr die Verse ein:

> *Liebchen, ach! Im starren Bande*
> *Zwängen sich die freyen Lieder,*
> *Die im reinen Himmellande*
> *Munter flogen hin und wieder.*
> *Allem ist die Zeit verderblich,*
> *Sie erhalten sich allein!*
> *Jede Zeile soll unsterblich,*
> *Ewig wie die Liebe seyn.*
>
> *1815.   1819.*

Eine gefühlvolle Widmung, gewiß. Aber hätte er nicht hier und ihr gegenüber deutlicher ihre ureigenen Gedichte erwähnen und vielleicht sogar dafür danken können? Die »freyen Lieder«, die »hin und wieder flogen«, sind wohl eine zu subtile Andeutung. An Willemer schrieb er zum Divan-Buch: »Möge indessen das Vergangene in die Gegenwart und der Freund in die nächste Nähe treten.« Nur ein einziges Mal kam Goethe Marianne gegenüber auf diese ihre Gedichte zu sprechen. Er teilte ihr mit, Eckermann habe in seinem Buch Beiträge zur Poesie gerade diese Gedichte erwähnt und die Strophen an den Westwind gewürdigt. »Wie oft hab ich nicht das Lied singen[5] hören«, schreibt Goethe an Marianne am 9. 5. 1824, »wie oft dessen Lob vernommen, und in der Stille mir lächelnd angeeignet, was denn wohl auch im schönsten Sinne mein eigen genannt werden dürfte.«

Im schönsten Sinn mein eigen. Was ist dieser schönste Sinn? Er durfte sich als Initiant fühlen, nur er hat Marianne zum Schreiben dieser Gedichte angeregt. Sie hat vor diesem Suleika-Jahr 1815 geschrieben, Gebrauchslyrik zu Geburtstagen und Familienfesten, sie schrieb auch nach diesem Jahr, aber eben kein Gedicht mehr solcher Dignität und Poesie. Ist dies jener »schönste Sinn«, wonach Goethe die Gedichte »mein eigen« nennen durfte? Marianne hat in einem Brief an Goethe vom Oktober 1819 ausführlich ihre Situation beschrieben:

> Es bleibt immer eine schwere Aufgabe, aus der Ferne und in die Ferne Gedanken und Worte zu senden, die nur in der nächsten Nähe gedeihen; das innige Gefühl spricht sich nur in vollendeter Form oder gar nicht aus, und wenn es heißt: ›Es sagt Dir ein beredtes Schweigen oft mehr als ein beredter Mund‹, – so setzt es allerdings eine erfreuliche Nähe voraus. Wenn ich diese allgemeinen Bemerkungen auf meine Lage anwende, so geht daraus hervor, daß ich eigentlich schweigen müßte, und durch die Entfernung gezwungen zu reden, will ich versuchen, ob sich schreibend beides vereinigen läßt.

> Ich habe den Divan wieder und immer wieder gelesen; ich kann das Gefühl weder beschreiben noch auch mir selbst erklären, das mich bei jedem verwandten Ton [ergriff]; wenn Ihnen mein Wesen und mein Inneres so klar geworden ist, als ich hoffe und wünsche, ja sogar gewiß sein darf, denn mein Herz lag offen vor Ihren Blicken, so bedarf es keiner

---

5 Alle drei von Goethe in den Divan aufgenommenen Gedichte von Marianne Willemer sind vertont worden: »Hochbeglückt in deiner Liebe« von Hugo Wolf u.a., das Westwind-Gedicht »Ach! Um deine feuchten Schwingen« von Felix Mendelssohn-Bartholdy, Franz Schubert und Karl Friedrich Zelter, das, Ostwind-Gedicht »Was bedeutet die Bewegung« von Mendelssohn und Schubert.

weitern ohnehin höchst mangelhaften Beschreibung. Sie fühlen und wissen genau, was in mir vorging, ich war mir selbst ein Rätsel; zugleich demütig und stolz, beschämt und entzückt, schien mir alles wie ein beseligender Traum, in dem man sein Bild verschönert, ja veredelt wieder erkennt, und sich alles gerne gefallen läßt, was man in diesem erhöhten Zustande Liebens- und Lobenswertes spricht und tut; ja sogar die unverkennbare Mitwirkung eines mächtigen höheren Wesens, insofern sie uns Vorzüge beilegt, die wir vielleicht gar nicht besitzen, und andere entdeckt, die wir nicht zu besitzen glaubten, ist in seiner Ursache so beglückend, daß man nichts tun kann, als es für eine Gabe des Himmels anzunehmen, wenn das Leben solche Silberblicke hat.

Marianne war sicher: Goethe mußte gefühlt haben, was in ihr vorging, gerade weil »ihr Herz offen« war. Sie selbst war sich bei diesem lyrischen Produktionsstrom »ein Rätsel«, es muß ein »erhöhter Zustand« gewesen sein, ja sogar die »unverkennbare Mitwirkung eines mächtigen höheren Wesens«. Es ist deutlich, Marianne hatte bei ihren »Silberblicken« kein Bewußtsein der Grenze zwischen Fiktion und Wirklichkeit, und nur deshalb konnte sie diese Gedichte schreiben und deshalb durfte Goethe sie »mein eigen« nennen: weil er im besonderen Sinn der »Urheber« war. Der Germanist Herman Grimm berichtet über eine Begegnung mit Marianne Willemer im Jahre 1850. Bei einem Spaziergang sei ein Wind aufgekommen und er, Grimm, habe sich an Goethes Gedicht »Westwind« erinnert und die Verse zitiert. Auf die Frage Mariannes, wie er dazu komme, antwortete er: »O, es fiel mir gerade so lebhaft ein, es ist eins von Goethes schönsten.« Da vertraute Marianne ihm ihr Lebensgeheimnis an, freilich mit der Bitte um Schweigen und Vertraulichkeit. Sie sahen sich wieder, Marianne legte Grimm die Dokumente vor, und dieser erkannte sofort die Bedeutung dieser Entdeckung, aber er behielt sie für sich, auch als Marianne als Sechsundsiebzigjährige am 6. Dezember 1860 starb.

Erst zehn Jahre nach ihrem Tod, 32 Jahre nach Goethes Tod und fünfzig Jahre nach Erscheinen des *Divan* schrieb Herman Grimm seine berühmte Studie *Goethe und Suleika*, 1869 in den Preußischen Jahrbüchern erschienen. Seitdem ist die Verfasserschaft zumindest dieser drei Gedichte klar.

Aber es bleibt die Frage, warum Goethe dies nicht selbst mitgeteilt hat, wieso er sich als Urheber auch dieser Gedichte empfand.

Die Frage zielt auf Goethes Produktionsweise in den letzten eineinhalb Jahrzehnten. Hatte er das Gefühl, mit den Realien des Lebens nicht mehr verbunden zu sein? Er nahm etwas wieder auf, was früher seine Übung war: Freunde und Bekannte zu bitten, ihre Tageserlebnisse aufzuschreiben und ihm diese Aufzeichnungen zu schicken. Johann Gottfried Herder hat dies schon früh (1789) kritisiert: »Hole der Henker den Gott, um den alles ringsumher eine Frage sein soll, die er nach seinem Gefallen braucht! Oder gelinder zu sagen: ich drücke mich weg von dem großen Künstler ... der auch seine Freunde und was ihm vorkommt, bloß als Papier ansieht, auf welches er schreibt.«

Seine unmittelbare Umgebung, Christiane, August, später die Sekretärin Caroline Ulrich, wurden angehalten, Briefe, Tagebücher, Tagesaufzeichnungen zu verfassen und ihm zu schicken. Goethes Tagebuch wird von ihm im ganzen als Konzept den Sekretären diktiert, die es dann schreiben. Caroline Ulrich soll einen ganzen Monat sein Tagebuch ohne sein Diktat geschrieben haben. Als der Sohn August vom Studium in Heidelberg zurückkehrt, muß er zwei Wochen warten, bis der Vater ihn empfängt, aber vorher muß er all seine Erlebnisse in einem Bericht festgehalten haben. Kennzeichnend ist Goethes Äußerung: »Wenn ich zwölf Söhne hätte, so schickte ich jeden an einen andern Ort, um an meinem eigen Fleisch und Bein zu erfahren, wie es überall aussieht.«

Goethe hat gelegentlich kleinere Texte von Dritten übernommen, doch es gibt keinen Parallelfall zu Mariannes *Divan*-Liedern. Eine Ausnahme ist das Gedicht »Nähe des Geliebten« mit dem Wortanfang der vier Strophen: »Ich denke dein«. In der ersten Aprilhälfte 1795 hörte Goethe bei der Familie Hufeland in Jena in der Vertonung von Zelter das Gedicht »Ich denke dein« von Friederike Brun. Die Melodie »hatte einen unglaublichen Reiz für mich, und ich konnte es nicht unterlassen, selbst das Lied dazu zu dichten, das in dem Schillerschen Musenalmanach steht«. Goethe übernahm den Stropheneinsatz »Ich denke dein«, änderte aber sonst den Text vollkommen.

Goethe war großzügig in der Übernahme der Beobachtungen und Erfahrungen anderer. Sicher war es für ihn selbstverständlich, daß Mariannes Gedichte einfach zu seinem »*Divan*« gehörten. Und verständlicherweise ist die Übernahme dieser Gedichte auch zu sehen im poetischen Überschwang der Gedichte und der Struktur des »Diwan« von Hafis.

Man muß in diesem Zusammenhang auf die »Bekenntnisse einer schönen Seele« hinweisen, die das umfangreiche 6. Buch von *Wilhelm Meisters Lehrjahre* bilden, ohne daß dort der Name der Urheberin fällt. Doch anders als im Fall der Gedichte Mariannes wies Goethe selbst in *Dichtung und Wahrheit* II,8 auf die Urheberin hin: »Aus deren Unterhaltungen und Briefen die Bekenntnisse der schönen Seele entstanden.« Man kann sicher sein, daß Texte von Susanna Katharina von Klettenberg die Grundlage für Goethes »Bekenntnisse« waren.

Eckermann berichtet (18. Januar 1825) von einem Gespräch über Originalität. Walter Scott habe eine Szene aus *Egmont* benutzt, und er hatte das Recht dazu. Lord Byrons verwandelter Teufel sei ein fortgesetzter Mephistopheles, und das sei recht. »So singt mein Mephistopheles ein Lied von Shakespeare, und warum sollte er das nicht? warum sollte ich mir die Mühe geben, ein eigenes zu erfinden, wenn das von Shakespeare eben recht war und eben das sagte, was es sollte?« Goethe spielt hier auf die Szene »Nacht. Straße vor Gretchens Türe« an. In Mephistos Lied »Was machst du mir / Vor Liebchens Tür« hat Goethe Verse aus dem ›Lied vom gefallenen Mädchen‹ (Hamlet IV5) eingefügt: »Er läßt dich ein / Als Mädchen ein, /Als Mädchen nicht zurücke.« Auf die Nachahmung Shakespeares kommt Goethe mit Kanzler von Müller zu sprechen, am 14. Februar 1824 über die »Zahmen Xenien« und noch einmal mit Bezug auf Faust am 17. Dezember 1824: »Gehört nicht alles, was die Vor- und Mitwelt geleistet, ihm [dem Schriftsteller] de iure an? Warum soll er sich scheuen, Blumen zu nehmen, wo er sie findet? Nur durch Aneignung fremder Schätze entsteht ein Großes. Hab' ich nicht auch im Mephistopheles den Hiob und ein Shakespearisches Lied mir ange-eignet?«

Goethes Produktionsweise ist ein hochinteressantes, von der Goethe-Forschung bislang vernachlässigtes Thema. Es kann hier nicht ausgeführt, sondern nur stichwortartig skizziert werden. Im »Historischen Teil« seiner *Farbenlehre* von 1810 reflektiert Goethe kulturkritisch die Unvermeidlichkeit der Aneignung fremder Stoffe und ihren Nutzen für die Gegenwart:

>»Niemals haben sich die Individuen vielleicht mehr vereinzelt und voneinander abgesondert als gegenwärtig. Jeder möchte das Universum vorstellen und aus sich darstellen; aber indem er mit Leidenschaft die Natur in sich aufnimmt, so ist er auch das Überlieferte, das, was andre geleistet, in sich aufzunehmen genötigt. Tut er es

nicht mit Bewußtsein, so wird es ihm unbewußt begegnen; empfängt er es nicht offenbar und gewissenhaft, so mag er es heimlich und gewissenlos ergreifen; mag er es nicht dankbar anerkennen, so werden ihm andere nachspüren: genug, wenn er nur Eigenes und Fremdes, unmittelbar und mittelbar aus den Händen der Natur oder von Vorgängern Empfangenes tüchtig zu bearbeiten und einer bedeutenden Individualität anzueignen weiß, so wird jederzeit für alle ein großer Vorteil daraus entstehen.« Das größte Genie käme nicht weit, wenn es alles nur ›aus sich‹ schöpfen wolle, bemerkt Goethe gegenüber Eckermann am 17. Februar 1832 (fünf Wochen vor seinem Tod): »Im Grunde aber sind wir alle kollektive Wesen, wir mögen uns stellen, wie wir wollen. Denn wie weniges haben und sind wir, das wir im reinsten Sinne unser Eigentum nennen! Wir müssen alle empfangen und lernen, sowohl von denen, die vor uns waren, als von denen, die mit uns sind. Selbst das größte Genie würde nicht weit kommen, wenn es alles seinem eigenen Innern verdanken wollte.«

Am selben Tag (!) trifft Goethe mit Hofrat Frédéric Jean Soret zusammen; Soret ist Naturfor- scher, Theologe und Schriftsteller aus Genf, er war von der Erbgroßherzogin Maria Pawlowna als Erzieher ihres Sohnes Karl Alexander nach Weimar berufen; Soret ist häufiger Gast bei Goethe und nimmt großen Anteil an seinen naturwissenschaftlichen Schriften. An diesem Tag sprechen sie über Mirabeau. Die Franzosen, so Goethe, wollten aus Mirabeau einen Herkules machen, aber auch ein Koloß bestünde nur aus Teilen. Was wäre denn das Genie, fragte Goethe, wenn ihm die Gabe fehlte, alles zu benutzen, was ihm auffällt. Dann (Soret zeichnete es in französischer Sprache auf: »Que suis-je moimême? Qu'ai-je fait? J'ai recueilli, utilisé tout ce que j'ai entendu, observé ...«): »Was bin denn ich selbst? Was habe ich denn gemacht? Ich sammelte und benutzte alles, was mir vor Augen, vor Ohren, vor die Sinne kam. Zu meinen Werken haben Tausende von Einzelwesen das Ihrige beigetragen, Toren und Weise, geistreiche Leute und Dummköpfe, Kinder, Männer und Greise, sie alle kamen und brachten mir ihre Gedanken, ihr Können, ihre Erfahrungen, ihr Leben und ihr Sein; so erntete ich oft, was andere gesäet; mein Lebenswerk ist das eines Kollektivwesens, und dies Werk trägt den Namen Goethe.«[6]

---

6 Goethe im Gespräch mit Frédéric Soret am 17. Februar 1832, in der Übersetzung von H. H. Houben (in der Ausgabe von 1929).

A House of Hope for Prudence and Harmony[1]

An interview with Daniel Barenboim
conducted by Wolfgang Behnken

Do you really believe that the Barenboim-Said Academy[2] can make a contribution towards a peaceful resolution of the Middle-East conflict?

Certainly not in the short-term – but in the long term, it's all the more likely. Look, when Edward Said and I founded the West-Eastern Divan Orchestra in 1999, 60 percent of the musicians had never played in an orchestra before, and 40 percent had never even heard a live orchestra concert. Eight years later, we played Arnold Schönberg's extremely difficult, highly complex 'Variations for Orchestra' in Salzburg – no one would have dared to predict that achievement. A development like that could take place in the Middle-East political conflict, too. It is a process that does not – or should not – exclude the hope for peace and reconciliation.

To what extent is there real harmony in the interaction between musicians of the West-Eastern Divan Orchestra?

They argue with each other, of course. And when they do, they work things out as in an independent republic, where compromises can and must be made. They have emancipated themselves from the ideological

---

1 This chapter in English, German and Arabic is reproduced here with the kind permission of the Barenboim-Said Akademie, Berlin.

2 In 1999, Daniel Barenboim and the American-Palestinian literary scholar Edward W. Said founded the West-Eastern Divan Orchestra in Weimar, Germany. The orchestra unites young Arab and Israeli musicians. Its name invokes J. W. Goethe's late, lyrical work, which reflects the German poet's admiration for the classical Persian love poems of Hafiz, as well as his study of Islamic culture over many years. From 2015 the Barenboim-Said Akademie, a music academy in Berlin, will begin educating up to 90 young musicians from the Middle East on scholarships, in the spirit of the West-Eastern Divan Orchestra. The will be enrolled in a four-year bachelor degree program in music, with a curriculum rooted in both music and the humanities. Headed by Daniel Barenboim, the academy will be housed in the former stage depot of the Staatsoper Unter den Linden, a conversion conversion project by the American Frank Gehry.

mindset of many of their parents and friends, in that they have listened to and maybe even accepted the other side's telling of the story. When an Israeli and a Syrian sit next to one another and play from the same page of music, and later eat together and talk, both experience something new. The Syrian, who had always assumed that all Israelis were enemies, hears the Israeli narrative for the first time. And he begins to understand that there is a certain logic to the Israeli perspective. The same is true for the Israeli, too, of course. The Orchestra is a living symbol of a better future in the Middle East. The musicians feel that just as I do, and for that reason they stick together.

Why are you founding your Academy in Germany rather than somewhere in the Middle East?

For one, because Berlin today is the music capital of the world. Additionally, the political situation in the Middle East makes it practically impossible to realize a project like this there. The situation is off-track, to put it mildly, but it's not hopeless. Many of our friends think of the Academy in Berlin as a utopian project. And that's true – but not every utopia has turned out to be a mistake. Just think of German Reunification. Perhaps you can think of the Academy as an unusual, even an unheard of attempt to support a political development by means of music. The goal of this political development is mutual understanding. Music is a universal language, and the word "enemy" is not in its vocabulary. The Federal Government of Germany and the City of Berlin, which both support this project – and I am grateful for their support – don't view it any differently. You see, I played in Ramallah for the first time for 200 Palestinian children, a girl came up to me, and I asked her, "are you happy I'm here?" I'll never forget her answer, "Yes, really happy. You are the first thing I've ever seen from Israel that wasn't a soldier or a tank." That's the way it was – she couldn't imagine Israelis as anything but uniformed objects, "things" or military vehicles. In the Academy, young Arabs and Israelis can and will overcome, and escape, this negative perspective on the world. And when they return to the homelands, they will take with them not just the experience of making music together, but also new friendships that cross borders. The Berlin Academy will be a house of hope for reason and harmony.

Is it possible that you are ascribing to music more power than it really has?

A symphony, a quartet, or an opera is not going to turn the world upside down; but music can change each and every one of us. And of course, music is powerful, because it is physical – it is a physical expression of the human soul, beyond the world of pure ideas. It calls into play every aspect of human existence: the brain, the heart, our moods. And every one of us reacts to music with all these aspects of our being. That makes music dangerous. Music is more powerful than words. And even in the saddest of compositions, there is a spark of hope within it. Because of that, music ties humanity together. Never in the history of our planet has so much music been heard as now. Music is the most beautiful form of globalization.

Do you think that Germany has a special role to play, maybe even that Germany must play a special role through its engagement with the Barenboim-Said Academy?

I have travelled all over the world ever since childhood. That was part and parcel of my career and my music-making. I am a citizen of Israel, of Spain, of Argentina, and of Palestine. And I know no other country that has dealt as intensively with its own history, and with its guilt about its own history, as Germany. In particular because of the Holocaust, maintaining good political and cultural relations with Israel is part of the creed on which the German state is founded – as every German chancellor up to now, and Chancellor Merkel, too, has emphasized. Germany therefore has an even more compelling interest in moderation and in finding a peaceful solution to the Middle-East conflict than other countries do. And without cooperation from all sides, such a solution is impossible. Sometimes I imagine a Middle-East conference that really contributes to peace in the region like a symphony played by graduates of our Academy in Berlin. A dream, certainly …

What would you play then?

Maybe Beethoven's Ninth, "He who knows the pride and pleasure // Of a friendship firm and strong …" But as long as we are talking about the special role of Germany – it is, after all, a kind of center in the world of music. There are more than 80 opera houses here, over 130 high-class orchestras – nearly a third of all professional symphony orchestras the world over – there is simply a vibrant legacy here of German and Austrian classicism, of the Romantic era, of modern music. And with every performance of Bach or Beethoven anywhere in the world, an idea of German culture, much more beautiful and sustainable than weapons exports, communicated to its audience. The great symphony orchestras are welcome representatives of Germany. And so are the 750 or so annual graduates of German music academies. Not all of them ultimately stay in Germany. The Academy's Arab and Israeli graduates will carry a new message with them back to their homelands – the message that mutual respect is not just possible, but necessary if people want to work together and live alongside each other in harmony. People are going to have to listen to them.

Ein Haus der Hoffnung auf Vernunft und Harmonie

Daniel Barenboim[1] im Gespräch mit Wolfgang Behnken

Glauben Sie wirklich, dass die Barenboim-Said Akademie einen friedensstiftenden Beitrag zur Lösung des Nahost-Konflikt leisten kann?

Kurzfristig bestimmt nicht, aber langfristig umso eher. Schauen Sie, als Edward Said und ich das West-östliche Divan Orchester im Jahr 1999 gründeten, hatten 60 Prozent der Musiker noch niemals in einem Orchester gespielt, und 40 Prozent hatten noch niemals ein Orchester live erlebt. Acht Jahre später haben wir in Salzburg Arnold Schönbergs äußerst schwierige, hochkomplexe »Orchester-Variationen« gespielt – niemand hätte sich getraut, das vorherzusagen. So ähnlich kann es auch in der Nahost-Politik zugehen – sie ist ein Prozess, der Hoffnung auf Frieden und Versöhnung nicht ausschließt. Oder nicht ausschließen sollte.

Wie harmonisch geht es denn zwischen den Musikern des West-Eastern Divan Orchestra zu?

Natürlich diskutieren sie miteinander. Es geht dabei zu wie in einer unabhängigen Republik, in der Kompromisse geschlossen werden können und müssen. Von der ideologischen Gedankenwelt mancher ihrer Eltern und Freunde haben sie sich emanzipiert, indem sie die Geschichte der

---

1 **Daniel Barenboim** is the General Music Director of the Staatsoper in Berlin, a post he has held since 1992. In 2011, he was appointed to the same position at La Scala in Milan. Born in Buenos Aires in 1942, Barenboim gave his first public concert at the age of seven in Buenos Aires, making his international debut as solo pianist in Vienna and Rome at the age of ten. Between 1975 and 1989, Daniel Barenboim acted as principal conductor of the Orchestre de Paris. From 1981 to 1999 he conducted in Bayreuth, and from 1991 to 2006 he was Music Director of the Chicago Symphony Orchestra. In Chicago the orchestra members named him honorary conductor, and in Berlin the Staatsoper unter den Linden appointed him principal conductor for life. Barenboim's 2006 Norton lectures at Harvard University have been published as *Music Quickens Time* and he is the co-author, with the late Edward Said, of *Parallels and Paradoxes: Explorations in Music and Society*.

jeweils anderen anhören und vielleicht auch akzeptieren. Beide, ob Israeli oder Syrer, die nebeneinander sitzen und vom selben Notenblatt spielen, die zusammen essen und reden, machen neue Erfahrungen. Der Syrer, der fest davon ausging, dass alle Israelis Mörder seien, hört zum ersten Mal das israelische Narrativ. Und er fängt an zu verstehen, dass der israelische Standpunkt eine gewisse Logik hat. Dasselbe gilt natürlich auch umgekehrt für den Israeli. Das Orchester ist ein lebendiges Symbol für eine bessere Zukunft im Nahen Osten. Das empfinden seine Musiker genauso wie ich, und darum halten sie zusammen.

Warum entsteht Ihre Akademie eigenlich in Deutschland und nicht irgendwo im Nahen Osten?

Zum einen, weil Berlin heute die Musikhauptstadt der Welt ist. Zum anderen, weil die politischen Verhältnisse in der Region ein solches Projekt dort nicht zulassen würden. Die Situation ist, gelinde gesagt, verfahren, aber nicht hoffnungslos. Manche unserer Freunde halten die Akademie in Berlin für ein utopisches Projekt. Das ist sie auch – aber nicht jede Utopie hat sich als Irrtum herausgestellt. Denken Sie nur an die Wiedervereinigung. Vielleicht kann man die Akademie als ungewöhnlichen, ja, unerhörten Versuch verstehen, mit den Mitteln der Musik eine politische Entwicklung zu befördern, an deren Ende gegenseitiges Verständnis steht. Musik ist eine universale Sprache, und Feindschaft gehört nicht zu ihrem Wortschatz. Nicht anders sehen es ja die Bundesregierung und die Stadt Berlin, die unser Vorhaben unterstützen, wofür ich sehr dankbar bin. Sehen Sie, als ich zum ersten Mal in Ramallah vor 200 palästinensischen Kindern spielte, kam ein Mädchen zu mir, und ich fragte sie: »Bist du froh, dass ich hier bin?« Ihre Antwort werde ich nie vergessen: »Ja, sehr. Sie sind das erste Ding aus Israel, das ich sehe, und das kein Soldat oder Panzer ist.« So war es – sie konnte sich Israelis nur als uniformierte Dinger oder Kampfwagen vorstellen. In der Akademie können und werden junge Araber und Israelis diese buchstäblich verdinglichte Weltsicht überwinden und ihr entkommen. Und wenn sie in ihre Heimatregionen zurückkehren, nehmen sie nicht nur Erfahrungen gemeinsamen Musizierens mit zurück, sondern auch neue Freundschaften, die über Grenzen reichen. Die Berliner Akademie wird ein Haus der Hoffnung auf Vernunft und Harmonie sein.

Könnte es sein, dass Sie der Musik womöglich zu viel Macht unterstellen?

Eine Sinfonie, ein Quartett oder eine Oper werden die Welt nicht umstürzen; aber verändern kann die Musik jeden Einzelnen von uns. Und natürlich ist sie mächtig, weil sie etwas Physisches ist, ein physikalischer Ausdruck der menschlichen Seele, jenseits der reinen Gedankenwelt. Sie greift alle Seiten des menschlichen Seins an: das Gehirn, das Herz, das Temperament. Und jeder von uns reagiert auf Musik mit allen diesen Seiten. Das macht sie gefährlich. Musik ist mächtiger als Worte. Und noch in der traurigsten Komposition ist ein Funke Hoffnung beschlossen. Weil das so ist, bindet sie die Menschheit zusammen. Noch nie in der Geschichte unseres Planeten wurde so viel Musik gehört. Sie ist die schönste Form der Globalisierung.

Glauben Sie, dass Deutschland mit der Barenboim-Said Akademie eine besondere Rolle spielen kann oder vielleicht sogar muss?

Ich bin in der Welt seit meiner Kindheit weit herumgekommen, das haben mein Beruf und die Musik so mit sich gebracht. Ich besitze die israelische, die spanische, die argentinische und die palästinensische Staatsbürgerschaft. Und ich kenne kein anderes Land, das sich derart instensiv mit seiner Geschichte, auch seiner Schuldgeschichte, so tief auseinandergesetzt hat wie Deutschland. Die Pflege guter politischer und kultureller Beziehungen zu Israel gehört zumal aufgrund des Holocaust zur deutschen Staatsräson, wie bisher jeder deutsche Kanzler und auch die Kanzlerin betont hat. Auch deshalb ist Deutschland an Mäßigung und einer friedichen Lösung des Nahost-Konflikts stärker interessiert als viele andere Staaten. Und diese Lösung ist ohne Kooperation der Beteiligten unmöglich. Manchmal stelle ich mir eine friedensstifende Nahost-Konferenz wie eine Sinfonie vor, gespielt von unseren Akademie-Absolventen aus Berlin. Ein Traum, gewiss.

Was würden Sie denn spielen?

Vielleicht Beethovens Neunte, »… wem der große Wurf gelungen, eines Freundes Freund zu sein«. Aber wenn wir schon von der besonderen Rolle Deutschlands sprechen – es ist ja eine Art musikalisches Weltzentrum. Hier gibt es mehr als 80 Opern, über 130 hochrangige Orchester, fast ein Drittel aller professionellen Kulturorchester der ganzen Welt, also ein lebendiges Erbe der deutschen und österreichischen Klassik, der Romantik und der musikalischen Moderne. Mit jeder Aufführung von Bach oder Beethoven im Ausland wird auch eine Idee deutscher Kultur in die Welt getragen, und das ist doch wesentlich nachhaltiger und schöner als Rüstungsexporte. Die großen Sinfonieorchester sind hochwillkommene Repräsentanten des Landes. Und die jährlich 750 Absolventen der deutschen Musikhochschulen sind es auch. Nicht alle bleiben schließlich in Deutschland. Unsere arabischen und israelischen Akademie-Stipendiaten werden eine neue Botschaft in ihre Heimatländer tragen, nämlich dass gegenseitiger Respekt möglich und nötig ist, um in Harmonie miteinander und nebeneinander zu arbeiten und zu leben. Man wird ihnen zuhören müssen.

حافظ، گوته و گينكو

نسيمى از اوراق ديوان جديد ۲۰۱۵–۲۰۱۹

حافظ و"غوته" وال"جنكة"

مصادر الإلهام للديوان الجديد ۲۰۱۵–۲۰۱۹

GINGKO
LIBRARY

کتابخانه گینکو
چاپ ۱۳۹۴ / ۲۰۱۵

ما هو الدیوان الجدید؟
باربرا هاوس شویبکه
ترجمة نیرمین النفرة

حافظ، آن قطرۀ محال اندیش
محمود دولت آبادی

آواز و آفریدن، ترانه و تنیدن، نغمه و نوید
یوهان ولفگانگ فون گوته
ترجمه رحیم غلامی

ما بر کرانۀ فرات
یواخیم سارتوریوس
ترجمه رحیم غلامی

دار الأمل للتعقل والإنسجام
مقابلة مع دانیال بارنبویم
ترجمة آران بیرن

فهرس المحتويات

ما هو الديوان الجديد؟

بدأ كلَّ شيءٍ بقصيدةٍ عن شجرة الجنكة، والتي ترجمتها أنثيا بيم ترجمةً جميلةً إحياءً لذكرى ويرنر مارك لينز عندما كان ألم فقدان هذا الرجل الملهم لا يزال في أوجه. أما بالنسبة لي، فإنَّ هذه القصيدة تمثل حياته أولاً كمؤسسٍ لدار كونتينيوم للنشر في نيويورك، وثانياً كمدير مؤسسة الجامعة الأمريكية للنشر في القاهرة.

الجنكة، تلك الشّجرة الشّرقية
في حديقتي نامية
وفي ورقتها سرّ من أسرار الحكمة بادية

هل هي واحدة وحيدة؟
أم منشطرة في ذاتها؟
وهل قرر شطراها أن تظهر واحدة لمن يراها

على أسئلة كهذه أجبت:
ألا تقول قصائد حبي في حال قد تساءلت
لِمَ أغني وحيداً ونحن اثنان؟

أرسل يوهان فولفغانغ فون غوته هذه القصيدة إلى صديقته الحبيبة ماريان فون ويلمر عربون محبةٍ. وألصق ورقتين جافتين بشكلٍ متقاطعٍ من هذه الشجرة تحت المقاطع الثلاث، وأرّخها في الخامس عشر من أيلول عام ١٨١٥. في هذا المجلد، يعيد النّاشر العظيم الرّاحل سيغفريد أنسيلد رواية قصة غوته وفون وشجرة الجنكة ببراعة.[1] وفي هذه المقدمة، يكفي أن نعرف أن غوته، وهو أعظم شعراء ألمانيا ومفكرًا وعالم طبيعة ورجل دولة ومواطناً عالمياً، كان قد اختار ورقة الجنكة كرمزٍ للأمل والحياة، والأهم من هذا كلّه فإن غوته اعتبر ورقة هذه الشجرة رمزاً للمشاعر العميقة والغامضة. فقد كانت هذه القصيدة نشيده الذي صاغه للتعبير عن صداقة ووحدة رمزية بين الشيخوخة والشباب، والمرأة

---

[1] في هذا المجلد، تظهر من ترجمة كينيث نورثكوت الانكليزية بموافقة دار جامعة شيكاغو للنشر، ومن النص الأصلي الألماني بموافقة دار زوركامب فيرلاغ للنشر.

والرجل، وبين ما هو دنيوي وما هو ديني، ومآبين الأدب والعلم، والشرق والغرب —وحدة كهذه كانت في نظر غوته غير قابلة للفصل:

اعرِف نفسك فحينها
ستعرِف الآخرَ وكذلك ترى
أنَّ المشرق والمغربَ
ليسَ لهما أن يفترقا أبدا

أصبحت هذه القصيدة جزءاً من الديوان الغربي-الشرقي، والذي استوحى غوته فكرة كتابته من قراءة الترجمة الألمانية للديوان الذي ألفه الشاعر الفارسيّ حافظ (خواجة شمس الدين محمد حافظ الشيرازي) في القرن الرابع عشر. فقد اعتبر غوته حافظ توأمه، وقرّر منذ ذلك الحين الدخول في حوار غنائي مع 'الآخر'. وتعني كلمة ديوان في اللغتين العربية والفارسية 'التجميع'، وقد جمع غوته ديواناً مؤلفاً من ١٢ مجلداً، وأطلق عليه اسم «نامه» وهي كلمة فارسية وتعني القصيدة الملحميّة. أضاف غوته جزءاً ثانياً لهذا المجلد بعنوان 'ملاحظات لِفهم أفضل'، والذي احتوى فصلاً بعنوان 'الديوان المُرتقب'، وذلك لأنّ غوته اعتبر أنّ ديوانه غير كامل، فقرّر أن يقدم في هذا الفصل اقتراحاً عن كيفية إكمال الديوان للشعراء والمفكرين الراغبين بذلك.

'في فترة زمنية معينة في ألمانيا، كانت العديد من المخطوطات تُوزّع للأصدقاء فقط، ولذلك فإن كلّ من كان يجد كتاباً غير جديرٍ بالقراءة، كان عليه أن يتذكّر أنّ الكتاب قد كتب لمن يتعاطف مع الكاتب فقط ، إضافةً إلى أصدقائه ومعجبيه. وعليه فقد قرّرت أن أُولّف ديواني الخاص، والذي اعتبره غير كامل بنسخته الحاليّة. ولو كنت أصغر سنّاً، لكنت قد أحجمت عن فعل ذلك، ولكن أعتقد أنّ الفرصة مواتيةٌ لأجمع هذا الديوان بدلاً من أن أعهد بهذه المهمة للأجيال القادمة تماماً كما فعل حافظ. وأنا على وشك أن أرسل هذا الكتاب تنتابني رغبة أن أكمله على أحسن وجه، ولذا قرّرتُ

أن أشير خطوةً خطوة وبالترتيب إلى ما يجب فعله لكي يكتمل هذا الكتاب'.

كان الديوان الغربي-الشرقي والذي نشر في عام ١٨١٩، محاولة غوته الجدّ شخصية لتوسيع أفق القرّاء الجاهلين والخائفين من المد الإسلامي. فمنذ زمن الحروب الفارسية والغرب يعتبر الشرق كياناً غريباً يشكل تهديداً مستمراً له، وهو ما قد ساهم بشكل أساسي في تشكيل الهويّة الغربيّة.

'لكلّ شيءٍ موسمه!' هذه الكلمات التي تم اقتباسها من كتاب 'سِفْر الجامعة' لغوته تفتتح مجموعة من المقالات التي تشكل جزءاً من الديوان الغربي-الشرقي. وها هنا نحن الآن نواجه عصراً آخر يشعر فيه الغربَ أنّ الإسلام يهدده. فالإسلام يمثّل بالنسبة له 'الآخر' وكل ما هو غامض ومجهول، وغالباً ما يتم الخلط بينه وبين التطرّف الديني. قال غوته أنّ 'لكل شيءٍ موسمه!'، ويبدو أن الوقت قد حان الآن لتأليف ديوان آخر، وهو ما سيعرف بالديوان الجديد.

لهذا الديوان الجديد بداية جليّة ونهاية سامية. ففي الخامس عشر من شهر أيلول لعام ٢٠١٥، وتزامناً مع مرور ٢٠٠ عام على إرسال غوته قصيدته إلى ماريان، فإنّ الشاعر والأمين العام السابق 'لمعهد غوته' يواخيم سارتوريوس سيجتمع مع الشاعر والكاتب والمترجم السوري أدونيس والكاتب المرموق محمود دولت آبادي لاختيار ١٢ شاعراً من الشرق و١٢ من الغرب ليدخلوا في حوار غنائيّ مع 'الآخر'. وستترجم أعمالهم إما عن طريق عملية ربط النصوص ببعضها أو من خلال ورش عمل يلتقي فيها الشعراء والمفكرون مع شعراء انكليز بهدف شرح النسخ الأصلية للقصائد، وبذلك سيصيغون شعراً جديداً أوحى به 'الآخر' مضافاً إليه حوار غنائيّ. وهذا ما سيشكل جوهر الديوان الجديد، والذي سيكون تجمعاً للشعراء

والمفكرين والمترجمين في أكاديمية سعيد وبارينبويم في برلين في عام ٢٠١٩، وهي الذكرى السنويّة لمرور ٢٠٠ عام على نشر الديوان الغربي-الشرقي.

ويُعتبر المجلد الذي نقرأه الآن مصدر وحيٍ لديوانٍ جديد. وتماماً مثل قصة الديوان الغربي-الشرقي فإنّ جزءاً منه أوحى به 'الآخر'، والجزء الآخر ما هو إلّا عبارة عن مقالات علمية 'لفهم أفضل'، وقصة ورقة الجنكة التي تنشطر إلى جزئين، ولكنّها تبقى ورقةً واحدةً، فإنّ هذا المجلد يضمّ الأعمال الأدبية الأصلية، كما يضمّ أيضاً ترجمة هذه الأعمال. يبدأ هذا المجلد بغزلٍ جميلٍ للشاعر حافظ، والذي ترجمته نرجس فرزاد، ولأنّه لا يحمل عنواناً مثل معظم القصائد الفارسيّة التقليديّة، فقد حمل اسم الكلمات الأولى التي ابتدأ بها: 'خدٌّ متوردٌّ'. يلي هذا الغزل مقالة بعنوان 'حافظ، القطرة التي تدرك ما يستحيل إدراكه'، والتي كتبها محمود دولت آبادي، وهو أحد أهم الروائيين في إيران. وتتناول هذه المقالة التي ألقيت في تجمع احتفالي للشعراء والمفكرين في فرانكفورت مسقط رأس غوته في ألمانيا في الذكرى المائة والخمسين لمولده أهمية شعر حافظ وأثره في الأدب. مارتن وير ورحيم غلامي ترجمت النص الأصلي إلى اللغة الإنجليزية، والتي تظهر في بداية الجانب الآخر من الكتاب.

وبما أنّ ترجمة جوزيف فون هامر برجشتال لديوان حافظ ألهمت الشاعر غوته ليكتب الديوان الغربي-الشرقي، فإنّه من المناسب أن نفتتح هذا الكتاب وحي لديوان جديد بقصيدة لحافظ وأخرى لغوته. وقد ألحقت قصيدة 'أغنية وشكل' لغوته بمقالة 'ونحن على ضفاف الفرات' التي كتبها يواخيم سارتوريوس، وفيها يشير إلى أن 'الدمج اللعوب لآداب أجنبية' تعد السمة المميزة في أعمال غوته الأخيرة: 'إنّ الدليل الجليّ على ذلك هو بلا شك الديوان الغربي-الشرقي لغوته. فالمغني في قصيدة "أغنية وشكل" في افتتاحية الديوان في

كتابه "المغني" يمثل غوته. وتُظهر قصائد هذا الكتاب نزوع الشاعر إلى العالم الشرقي وحماسه وارتباطه به'.

إنّ يواخيم سارتوريوس مفكرٌ وشاعرٌ في الوقت ذاته، ولذلك فهو كورقة الجنكة التي تنشطر إلى جزئين. وكابن لدبلوماسي كان على يواخيم أن يتعرّض 'للآخر' في سن مبكرة مما أثرّ في كتاباته. فقصيدته 'في أسلوب أبي نواس'[2] تُعدّ مثالاً على الحوار الغنائيّ الذي يشكل جوهر الديوان الجديد. ويُعتبر أبو نواس من أعظم الأدباء العرب ومصدر إلهام العديد من الشعراء الفرس الكلاسيكيين أمثال عمر الخيام وحافظ، بالإضافة إلى عدد من الشعراء المعاصرين كيواخيم سارتوريوس، وكتّاب الخيال الشعبي مثل أندرو كيلين.

وقد تلت قصيدة 'في أسلوب أبي نواس' قصيدة 'الصحراء' لأدونيس، وهي جزءٌ من ديوانه الشعري ثنائي اللغة ضحايا خريطة.[3] ويُعدّ الشاعر السوري علي أحمد والمعروف في الوسط الأدبي بأدونيس أحد أهم الشعراء المعاصرين في العالم العربي، وهو أول من ترجم كتاب التحولات لأوفيد، ولذلك فهو يمثل عنصراً هاماً في الحوارات الغنائية التي بدأها حافظ وغوته. وديوانه الشعر العربي، والذي يضم أعمالاً شعريةً تغطي ما يقارب الألفي عام، ما يزال يطبع في دور النشر منذ إصدار الطبعة الأولى في عام ١٩٦٤.

ولكي يحقق الديوان الجديد النجاح فلا بدّ للشعراء أن يستوعبوا 'الآخر' ويقدّروا أعمالهم، ومن هنا تأتي أهمية ترجمة هذه الأعمال الأدبية، وهي عملية ليست بسهلة كما أكد الشاعر الهندي ماكارند بارانجاني:

نعم، ما يودّ قوله إن ترجمة الشعر لن تكون بالسّهلة

---

[2] ويظهر في هذا المجلد كلُّ من النص الأصلي الألماني الذي نشرته دار كيبنهاير وفتش، والتأويل الذي قدمه كريستوفر ميدلتون في اللغة الانكليزية بموافقة دار كاركنيت للنشر.
[3] ترجمها عبد الله الأضحري، وظهرت في هذا المجلد بموافقة دار الساقي للطباعة والنشر.

٥

وكيف لها، إن كانت القصيدة ذاتها ترجمة
لمشاعر إما تكون رقيقة بالكاد تشعر بها
أو قوية ليس بالمقدور كبحها؟

يتضمن هذا المجلد أيضاً قصيدة من المجلد الأول الذي أصدرته مجلة 'الشعر الحديث في
الترجمة' في عام ٢٠١٥، والذي يركز على الأدب الإيراني، وتم إصداره بالتعاون مع المجلس
الثقافي البريطاني كجزء من برنامج 'موسم الثقافة البريطاني الإيراني'. وقد قام الشاعر
والمترجم هيوبرت مور بالتعاون مع نسرين برفاز بترجمة قصائد سابير هاكا حرفياً.

ومنذ عصر حافظ وحتى الآن، أصبح الشعراء شوكة في نحور الجبابرة. ويبدأ جزء الشعر في
مجلد 'الوحي' بترجمة نرجس فرزاد الجميلة لشعر حافظ، وتصف نرجس أهمية الشعراء
للشعب الإيراني قائلةً:

'يُذكّر الشعراء دائماً السلطة الحاكمة أنّ القوة قد تفسد النفوس، وأن
الإيرانيين على قناعة منذ أيام الشاه نامه أنّه لا يمكن لأحد أن يحتكر
السلطة في إيران. وبالطبع فإنّ الشعراء يقومون بذلك مهارة وجمال، فهم
يغلّفون المعنى في القصيدة بعدة طبقات لتصبح القصيدة شبيه بعجينة
الرقائق، ولذا فإنّه يتوجب عليك إزالة الطبقات الواحدة تلو الأخرى لتصل
إلى جوهر الموضوع. وقد ذكر أحد الشعراء المعاصرين المفضلين لدي، والذي
توفّي في أوائل الثمانينات، أنّ الشعراء هم ورثة الماء والحكمة والضوء.
ويشير الماء إلى الزمان الذي أضاف إليه الشعراء من حكمتهم ونورهم
فأناروا طريقنا لأنهم أنبياء زماننا'.[٤]

وكانت الترجمة الفكرة الرئيسية لمقالة في مجلد 'الوحي'. وفي هذه يصف الشاعر والمفكر
إريك أورمسبي عملية ترجمة 'ملاحظات لفهم أفضل' للشاعر غوته لقرّاء معاصرين. إنّ
محور الوحي لديوان جديد هو مقابلة أجريت مع مؤسس 'أوركسترا الديوان الغربي-
الشرقي' دانييل بارينبويم، وفيها يتحدث المايسترو عن 'أكاديمية سعيد وبارينبويم' حيث

http://www.bbc.co.uk/programmes/b01kjs1j[٤]

سيعقد الديوان الجديد في عام ٢٠١٩ ليبدأ الحوار بين الشعراء والمفكرين على أمل أن يقود حوارٌ مبنيٌّ على الاحترام المتبادل إلى فهمٍ أفضلَ 'للآخر'. وقد أُستخدم نص هذه المقابلة في هذا المجلد في لغات ثلاث: الألمانية والانكليزية والعربية وذلك بموافقة الأكاديمية. هذا وتفتتح النسخة العربية من هذه المقابلة الجزء الذي يحتوي النص الأصلي لمقالة محمود دولت آبادي عن حافظ في اللغة الفارسية، وتعليق يواخيم سارتوريوس على الديوان الغربي-الشرقي لغوته مترجم إلى الفارسية. كما يحتوي هذا الجزء أيضاً هذه المقدمة مترجمة إلى العربية.

باربرا هاوس شوييكه
١٥ أيلول ٢٠١٥
ترجمة نيرمين النفرة

v

حافظ،

آن قطرهٔ محال اندیش[1]

سال ۱۹۹۹ میلادی مصادف بود با دویست و پنجاهمین سالگرد تولد گوته، به این مناسبت در روز ششم شهریور ماه سال ۱۳۷۸ مراسمی در شهر فرانکفورت آلمان برگزار شد، محمود دولت آبادی نمایندهٔ برحق اهل قلم این سرزمین کهنسال در این مراسم حضور یافت و در بزرگداشت گوته آن حافظ شناس و شاعر بلند آوازهٔ آلمانی، درباره لسان الغیب سخنانی ایراد کرد. در این جشن بزرگ، پیتر یوستینف دربارهٔ ویلیام شکسپیر، جولیاس ماریاس در مورد قلم و قدرت کلام سروانتس، جُرج گُراد در باب شعر شاندر پتوفی، محمود دولت آبادی، در زمینهٔ نقش و نفوذ غزل حافظ، ویکتور گروف در حوزهٔ حیات و شعر الکساندر پوشکین، و زیگفرید لنس در احوال و آثار ولفگانگ گوته، سخنرانی کردند.

گفتنی است که متن سخنرانی ها پیش از زمان برنامه به زبان آلمانی ترجمه و در جزوه ای چاپ شده بود، مترجم متن سخنرانی دولت آبادی دکتر بهمن نیرومند بوده است. همچنین روزنامهٔ معتبر فرانکفورتر اَلگمـاینه در بخش ویژه ای از محمود دولت آبادی، زیگفرید لنس و جرج گُراد به عنوان سه سخنران برتر یاد کرد. برنامه بزرگداشت گوته در تالار شهر فرانکفورت برگزار شد، و علاوه بر سخنرانان اصلی، ملکه صوفی از اسپانیا جزو مدعوین بوده و خانم پتراروت شهردار شهر فرانکفورت، میزبان مسئول و خانم یوتارا بِه لینگ وزیر آموزش عالی استان هِسِن، میزبان ویژهٔ بخش ایران و میز-تریبون حافظ بود.

محمود دولت آبادی با سخن تازهٔ خود دربارهٔ خواجه شیراز با عنوان «حافظ، آن قطرهٔ محال اندیش» نگاهی دیگر به لسان الغیب داشته است که مقدمهٔ متن و اصل سخنرانی را می خوانید:

بوالعجب کاری!

بی گمان خواجه شمس الدین محمّد حافظ یک بار دیگر در روزگار ما کشف شده است و این کار بسیار ظریف و مهم به برکت فرهیختگانی چون محمدعلی فروغی، جناب دکتر قاسم غنی (همشهری دانشور من) جناب دکتر فیاض، زنده یاد دکتر پرویز ناتل خانلری، شادروان انجوی، استاد مطهری، آقایان زرین کوب، شاهرخ مسکوب و اساتید من جناب شاملو و ابتهاج، و دوستان دانشمندم آقایان داریوش آشوری و بخصوص جناب بهاءالدین خرمشاهی که حافظ پروژه و قرآن پژوه نامی روزگار ماست، صورت گرفته است. توجه و پرداختن شخصیّت هایی چنین فاضل و

---

[1] نخستین چاپ: مهرماه ۱۳۷۸.

۹

صاحب نظر و بسیاری از دیگر هموطنان ما به «حافظ» خود نشان دیگری است بر اهمیت حافظ در زبان، اندیشه و خُلق و خوی و رفتار ما ایرانیان، و کوشش همهٔ اساتید از آن جهت باید مورد قدرشناسی ما قرار بگیرد که موجبات آشنایی بیش‌تر، از زوایای گوناگون را برای ما — هنرپذیران — فراهم آورده است و فراهم می‌آورد. به این اعتبار و با چنین قدرشناسی عمیق و صمیمانه‌ای است که من هم از چشم‌انداز خودم در جهان‌بینی، ریخت‌مندی و خم‌وچم زبان خواجه نگاه کرده‌ام، و خوشبختانه آن «رند قرعه بر غم زده» — حافظ — چنان مجموعهٔ پیچیده و بی‌تمامی است که از هر گوشه‌ای می‌توان به او قربت یافت. آنچه می‌ماند زمان کوتاه در بزرگداشت گوته است برای معرفی حافظ — حداکثر ۱۵ دقیقه برای هر سخنران — و من چندی دچار این مشکل بودم که چگونه بحر را در کوزه‌ای بگنجانم؛ و سرانجام آنچه استاد ازل گفت بگو من نوشتم؛ چنان فشرده و چکیده که بایسته بود و امیدوارم به توفیقی اندک دست یافته باشم در این مهم، با عزت و احترام به همهٔ حافظ‌شناسان و حافظ‌دوستان سرزمینم و به یاد پدرم، آن رند بلاکش که با ما سخن نمی‌داشت مگر از زبان حافظ و سعدی و فردوسی.

حافظ، آن قطرهٔ محال‌اندیش

حافظا!

«شخص باید دیوانه باشد، تا خود را با تو برابر بینگارد.»

گوته: دیوان غربی-شرقی

"در ازل پرتو حُسنت ز تجلّی دم زد — عشق پیدا شد و آتش به همه عالم زد

جلوه‌ای کرد رُخت دید مَلَک عشق نداشت — عین آتش شد از این غیرت و بر آدم زد"[1]

چنین است جهان‌بینی حافظ:

آفرینش در عشق، از عشق و برای عشق. روشن شدن، برافروختنِ هستی در شکفتن نخستین. «فرشته عشق نداند که چیست!»[2] پس، آدم موضوعیت عشق آمد و آن درخشش جاودانه در «آدم» گرفت، و آدم به صورت آفریدگار خود «بار امانت» را به وجدان برگرفت؛ اندوه و دغدغهٔ ازلی-

---

[1] "عقل می‌خواست کزان شعله چراغ افروزد — برق غیرت بدرخشید و جهان برهم زد
مدعی خواست که آید به تماشاگهِ راز — دست غیب آمد و بر سینهٔ نامحرم زد
دیگران قرعهٔ قسمت همه بر عیش زدند — دلِ غمدیدهٔ ما بود که هم بر غم زد
جان عُلوی هوسِ چاه زنخدانِ تو داشت — دست در حلقهٔ آن زلف خم اندر خم زد
حافظ آن روز طربنامهٔ عشق تو نوشت — که قلم بر سرِ اسبابِ دل خرّم زد".
[2] آنچه بین گیومه می‌آید: بیت، مصراع یا جمله یا کلمه، برگرفته از حافظ است، مگر در پانویس نام گوینده یا شاعر دیگری قید شود.

ابدی: هستی و شدن در مسیرِ ناممکنِ کمال، حقیقت. گذر از آزمونی سخت برای رسیدن، رسیدن به اصل: همه «او» شدن. در نظر حافظ «عقل» برای درک هستی، ظرف خردینه ای ست؛ زیرا حرکت و جنبش هستی به «عشق» است و هم با عشق و اشراق می توان در آن حضور داشت و «هست» بود.

گوته با معیار غزل حافظ، برای شعر چهار اصل قائل می شود: عشق؛ می گلگون؛ پیروزی امید؛ ستیختن با زشتی[1] — با ترکیب و تناسبی چنان موزون که چون کلام حافظ دلنشین باشد و جاودان بماند.

باید گفت درکی چنین عمیق از حافظ به واسطه زبان دوم، شگفت آور و تحسین برانگیز است. امّا من همچنان تردید دارم که یک خوانندهٔ عادی بتواند حافظ را جز در زبان فارسی، آن هم به تدریج و در مسیر عمر عمیقاً درک کند.

زیرا جان هیچ انسانی را گنجایش پیوسته این همه انباشت معانی، کشف زیبایی، ناپرابستی عشق و نازکای حکمت نیست.

پس غزل حافظ را بهتر است همچنان خواند که سروده شده است؛ به تدریج و در مسیر بیش از نیم قرن؛ بارها خواندن حافظ اگر به نیاز خوانده شود، هرگز حس تکرار در انسان ایجاد نمی کند، که در هر بار خوانشِ خلاّقهٔ او نکتهٔ تازه ای به دست توان آورد.

به راستی «چه هاست در سرِ این قطرهٔ محال اندیش؟»

باری ... خواجه حافظ — حافظ قرآن کریم با قرائت در چهارده روایت — شمس الدین محمّد — آن که خود را قطره ای در هستی می شمرد تا ناممکن های آن بیاندیشد، در قرن هشتم هجری شمسی در شیراز بزاد، هم در آن قرن فرمان یافت. هفتاد سال به دنیا عمر کرد و کم تر از پانصد غزل به خود به یادگار گذاشت که نخستین بار ۳۵ سال بعد از درگذشت خواجه، گردآوری و در یک دفتر (دیوان) مکتوب شد. نوشته اند پیش از آن، بخصوص در بودیِ حافظ کسی را جسارت آن نبودی تا سر در این کار کند.

در عمر حافظ، دوبار کتابشویان و کتابسوزان در شیراز به نمایش گذاشته شد به بهانهٔ خوانده شدن کُتبِ فلسفی. یک بار در حکومت امیر مبارزالدین، و یک بار در حکومت پسر و جانشین او شاه شجاع که هر دو امیر خراج گزار ایلخانان مغول بودند و هم یوغ بیعت با ته ماندهٔ خلفای عباسی (در مصر) را بر گردن داشتند. امیر مبارز که نه خیلی دیر به دست پسرش کور شد، چنان در تعصب و ریا عرصه را بر مردم تنگ کرده بود که به او لقب «محتسب» داده بودند و زندگی پنهان،

---

[1] گوته، دیوان غربی-شرقی.

«شیوه رندان بلاکش» شده بود. او تدریس فلسفه را در مدارس ممنوع کرده بود. مفتی ها و شیوخ خانقاه را برکشیده، دانشوران آزاده را منزوی کرده، از بزرگ صوفیان مِلّاکی کلان ساخته بود و بزرگ ترین امام شهر (چنان که نوشته اند) از زاویه خود بیرون نمی آمد، مگر جمعه ها برای نماز جماعت، و شبانه روز دهان روزه — هزار رکعت نماز می گزارد. کرسی قضاوت از طریق مزایده دست به دست می شد[۱] و ... «قاضی را هیچ آفریده پیش نخواند ... و هر که، برابر و روی در روی قاضی سخنان سخت گوید و جواب دهد و حرمت او کم کند، فرمودیم شحنهٔ ولایت او را سزا دهد!» و ... «تزویر و تلبیس و مکر و حرامخوارگی و ظلم و بهتان ... گواهی به دروغ ... حیلت و افساد در میان خلق، بی شرمی و اخذ رشوت!»[۲] خصیصه اخلاق اشراف روزگار بود، و مردمان ضمن تحمل جباریت حکام، از بیم اُطراق پیوستهٔ ایلچیان مغول، خانه نو نمی کردند و در خانه های رو به ویرانی خود مرده دفن می کردند شاید ایلچیان از نحسی برمند و وارد نشوند، که وارد می شدند و می طلبیدند: آذوقه، علوفه، سفره، شراب و شاهد هم!

«مقام پیران و عبادتگاه پاکان»

چنین بود لقب شهر شیراز، و امیر مبارز، به تقلید خلفا، جمعه ها پیاده به نماز جماعت می رفت.

***

من در جوانی تاریخ سرزمین خود را خواندم و چنان دلزده و افسرده شدم که یکسره خود را غرق کردم در وجد و اندوه ادبیات، زیرا از تمام تاریخ بوی جنایت بلند بود و صدای چکاچاک جهل با جهل، و فرو ریزش شأن و ارزش آدمی در انهدام اندیشه و زیبایی و آزادی.

امّا ... چنانچه از 'دیوان غربی-شرقی' بر می آید، گوته فرزانه شیفته و افسونِ کمال زیبایی معانی و بیان در غزل حافظ می شود. از همان چشم انداز هم به زیبایی های خیال انگیز شرق می رسد. و از برکت چنین درکی به ضرورت و نیاز نزدیکی فرهنگی شرق با غرب که حافظ روشن ترین دریچه و خجسته ترین انگیزه این آشنایی ست.

زیرا حافظ نه فقط میراث دار سعدی، که وارث کمال یافتهٔ زبان پارسی دری ست. زبانی که با رودکی شکفته شد، در حکیم فردوسی به ظرفیت های حماسی خود دست یافت و در نظامی به امکانِ غنایی اش؛ این زبان، که در بیان موجز عارفان به زلالی ناب رسیده بود، در مولوی گداخته و در سعدی پرداخته شد و اکنون حافظ قُله بَرین زبانی بود که در ذات خود سوادِ ارزش های لگدمال شدهٔ یک قوم قدیمی را پاس می داشت با هر غزل، هر بیت و هر واژه که او همواره کامل ترین تراش الماس آن را در نگین «انگشتر سلیمانی» خود می نشاند. حافظ دانش مَدرسی را

---

[۱] شد الازار، روایت مرحوم انجوی.
[۲] جامع التواریخ، خواجه رشید الدین فضل الله.

۱۲

آموخته، «درس سحر در ره میخانه نهاده بود» و «شیوهٔ رندی» در پیش گرفته. او زبان و شعر عرب را می دانسته و می شناخته؛ و موسیقی و آواز را هم. امّا دانش او منحصر به معارف و ادبیات بعد از اسلام نمی ماند. چنانچه درونمایه های عهد عتیق و عهد جدید، نشانه هایی از مهر پرستی، مانویت، آیین زرتشتی؛ نیز اسطوره و تاریخ و نجوم و مایه هایی از دانش فلسفی یونان ... در غزل حافظ بازتاب هنرمندانه می یابند. می و معشوق و ساقی و شاهد و مطرب و یار و جانان و مغ و مغان و رند و پیر و سالک در مجموعه شیخ و زاهد و صوفی و شحنه و محتسب و غیره، با عملکردی مغایر شخصیت های نمادین در غزل حافظ اند.

خورشید، نور، روشنایی، مهتاب، سحر، سپیده، طلوع و طلعت و طالع مفاهیم و نمادهای ازلی حافظ اند که همواره در مقابله و تعارض با تاریکی، ظلمت[1]، نومیدی، ریاکاری، بدعهدی و غدر زمانه قرار می گیرند ...

و بوی خوش! زبان خواجه معطر است: آغوشمال در گل و بهار و نسیم؛ و به رنگ مهتاب و می ارغوان که یکجا نثار دوست می شود، معشوق یا معبود:

«رواق منظر چشم من آشیانه توست — کرم نما و فرود آ که خانه، خانهٔ توست»

غزل حافظ در لحظاتی به خیال خوش گذشته باز می گردد، به «شهریاران» و «شهرِ»-«یاران» در «جام جهان نمای» خسروانه ای که دیگر نیست؛ امّا بیش از آن حضور گذشته در غزل حافظ همچون وجدان پاره پاره و گمشده جمعی ما، بازتاب کلیت و کلیات روحی یک قوم است همچون امری اجتناب ناپذیر.

به لحاظ ریخت شناسی هنری نیز، حافظ بازتابندهٔ جوهر جغرافیایی-محیطی، و روحیه نهفته در طبیعت معماری قدیم ایران قدیم نیز هست! چنانچه به لحاظ شخصیتی-شخصیت شناسی، او تجسم واقعیت محضِ انسان فرهیخته ایرانی ست و کاملاً یگانه با روحیهٔ جغرافیایی-اقلیمی ایران. یعنی آن منش «چمانی» استبداد آزموده که در انعطاف پذیری و کمانگی معنا می پذیرد و لقب «رند» از او پدید می آید. با چنین دریافتی ست که لحن، بیان و حتی واژگانِ حافظ را هلالی، کمانی، مواج و سپرنده (سپری شونده) می توان دید. مثل امواج رمل، مثل گرده ماهی های مواج شدن، و مثل قرینه سازی ها در تاق و دربندها. و این تاق و هشتی و درگاه و دالان و رَف و دریچه و تاقچه، آن اندرونی و بیرونی و قوس ها در بام های گنبدی-گهواره ای؛ آن سقف و ایوان و کنگره و عرش، و پستو-پسله ها و فضاهای تو در تو که به ابهام می انجامد و خصیصه ای روانی-اعتقادی را باز می تاباند (خصیصه ای پنهان پوش و درون گرا) چرا نباید بازتاب ناب و درخشانِ خود را در غزل بیابد، حتی در ضرب و مکث های فواصل هر جمله؟

---

[1] "صحبت حکام، ظلمت شب یلداست — نور ز خورشید جوی، بو که برآید".

«گل در بر و می در کف و معشوق به کام است!»

بی‌گمان خوانندۀ عادی کنجکاو «از کجا آمد؟» کلام خواجه نیست؛ چون جمیع یادهای قومی و ناپیدای حافظ را در وجدان جمعی خود دارد. همین است اگر انسان ایرانی خود را هم‌پیوند حس می‌کند با هم‌زبان خود حافظ که توانسته است مجموعۀ تعارضات تاریخی-آیینی یک مردم را در اعتدال و با مراعات، به وحدت و آشتی بکشاند؛ و خود بی‌قرار و بی‌آرام در حد فاصل سخیف ترین روزمَرّگی ها تا دورترین مفاهیم آرمانی، تا رسیدن به «آن گِرد نگونسار فیروزه ای» با نظم هماهنگ موسیقایی هستی، در شدن و شدن باشد؛ چنان که گویی آن رندِ «قرعه بر غم زده» از خم باریک کوی کاهگلی پا برون می‌کشد تا رها شود در مدار هستی، تا در آغاز که:

«عشق پیدا شد و آتش به همه عالَم زد».

***

باری ... حافظ را به محکمۀ تفتیش عقایدش هم بردند، از «بخل» امّا به بهانۀ شک؛ و در آن گیر و دار زنان خانه همۀ دستنوشته های او را شستند و پاره کردند.

خواری عشق، آری. خوار شماری عشق:

«جای آنست که خون موج زند در دلِ لعل — زین تغابن که خزف می شکند بازارش»

بسیار اندیشیده‌ام به این که آیا چه مفهومی در ذهنیات و روحیات انسانی وجود دارد که حافظ به آن نپرداخته باشد؟ و کدام واژه هست که در به جاترین جای خود، در زبان حافظ نیامده باشد؟ و کدام سؤال درونی انسانی هست که حافظ به آن نیندیشیده باشد؟ نمی توان گفت بی تحول باقی ماندن زبان فارسی باعث استقبال خاص و عام از غزل حافظ بوده است. نه؛ زبان فارسی بی‌تغییر هم نمانده است و بخصوص باید توجه داشت که خواندن حافظ، هیچ آسان نیست. امّا رمز زبانِ حافظ این است که دست رد بر سینه هیچ نیازمندی نمی زند. همگان محرم ذهن و زبان خواجه اند، و از «بحری» که اوست آب می توانند برداشت. مردم از هر بابی و دربارۀ هر مشکلی با حافظ مشورت می کنند؛ در عشق و در اندوه و در شکست و درماندگی، در شوریدگی و انکار و در ایمان و امید و در دام و در رهایی؛ و در باور ما ایرانیان حافظ لسان الغیب خوانده می شود. زبانی که بی پاسخ ات رها نمی کند. حافظ انباشتِ معانی همواره بدیع است و خود نیز بدان اشارت ها دارد. چنین لقبی به خواجه دادن هم، نشانۀ حس و درک رازوارگی زبان و بیانِ حافظ است از جانب وجدان جمعی ما. آن رمز و رازها که در ساختار و در معنا، فوَرانی و در دوَرانی است، چرخنده و گریزنده، همه سویه، واحد و متکثّر — مثل کائنات — و در همه حال امیدبخش از اعماق نومیدی ها.

از سوی دیگر حافظ نماد گُنجاهای جانِ فرهیختهٔ انسان ایرانی‌ست در گذر از آزمون‌های سخت با ظرافت‌های انعطاف‌پذیر مینیاتوری، در تحمل و تأمل، و در نگاه سپنجی خیامی به دنیا، در باریک‌بینی و انعطاف و تساهل، در قناعت و بلندنظری و بلندهمتی، و در بی‌اعتنایی به دنیا و دنائت‌های دنیایی[1]. نور ز خورشید جوی بلکه برآید.

دیگر ... و آشکارترین علت گرایش به حافظ شباهت بسیار نزدیک شرایط روزگار حافظ است با شرایط بعد از او تا بعد و بعد و بعدتر ... که ای بسا سخیف‌تر و شنیع‌تر شده است؛ چندان که در تالابِ قرونِ بعد از عصر حافظ، حتی نیلوفری هم نرویید. از آن که ظلمت چیره‌تر شد. به این سبب حافظ تاركِ غزل پارسی و هم پایانِ شکوهمند آن شمرده می‌شود. بعد از حافظ ذلت و انحطاط و زوال چنان عمق و گستره‌ای می‌یابد که گمان توان برد خواندنِ حافظ هم امری آسان نبوده باشد. پس ظرافت طبع انسان ایرانی، انسانی که در هر مقطع و دوره‌ای به درونِ خود واپس رانده می‌شود، چگونه می‌تواند از حافظ، همدل و همزبان خود، فاصله بگیرد و او را از خود دور بدارد؟ سهل است که چگونه می‌تواند او را، این ذهنیت همیشهٔ یک ملت را مثل گوهر حقیقت در وجدان پریشان خود، نستاید؟ آخر حافظ امید لحظاتِ مرگبار هر انسان ایرانی بوده است و هست، با این ظرفیت برتر که او در اوج‌های وجد و امید هم دست‌افشانِ میدان‌های شادمانی و زندگی توانسته است باشد؛ که او در همه‌حال ستیزندهٔ با زشتی‌ست و ستایندهٔ زیبایی. و زبان عشق است از زمینی‌ترین و دستیاب‌ترین عشق تا دورترین مفهوم هستی شناسانهٔ آن. که یعنی عشقِ به اصل خود، به گوهر آفرینش.

***

باری ... نبوغ حافظ، آن «قطرهٔ محال اندیش»، غزل حافظ است در خلاقه‌ترین وجه بیان و غنای معنا. امّا معجزهٔ حافظ به گمان من زیستن اوست در ورطه‌های عشق و هلاک: ایستادن و درنیفتادن-خمیدنِ گندم‌وار و باز ایستادن و نشکستن، تا سهمی از آن «بارِ امانت»[2] را که بر عهده گرفته بود، به منزل برساند و — انصاف را — به منزل هم رسانید؛ از آن که:

«کس چو حافظ نگشاد از رخ اندیشه نقاب — تا سرِ زلف عروسانِ سخن شانه زدند.»

محمود دولت‌آبادی
۱۸ مرداد ماه ۱۳۷۸، تهران

---

[1] "ارچه گردآلود فقرم، شرم باد از همّتم —گر به آبِ چشمهٔ خورشید دامن تَر کنم".
[2] "آسمان بار امانت نتوانست کشید — قرعهٔ فال به نام من دیوانه زدند".

آواز و آفریدن، ترانه و تنیدن، نغمه و نوید

یوهان ولفگانگ فون گوته

ترجمهٔ رحیم غلامی

بگذار یونانی بسرشتِ گِل خود پردازد،

و از آن صورتی از نور برون افرازد!

بگذار که آن کودکِ دستان خودش

برکشد، در خلقِ تحیّر، پیکرش را در سماع!

در دیدهٔ ما، اوج آرامش و سرور

اینست که درآییم در فُرات،

در تک آب ذَوات، پس و پیش تشنهٔ شاخ نبات!

و با آوازی چون آب حیات،

بر عنصر سیّال، بگذریم از ممات!

آتش جان من آرام گیرد، گر نام شما

بِماند در حرفْ حرفِ هر نوآ

تا آواز بر آفریدن، ترانه بر تنیدن، نغمه بر نوید، جمله دارند ندآ

دست توانای شاعر می‌آفریند شعر ز آب،

چون گوی معلّق بر سما!

همو که در دیوان شعر،

می‌نهد می ارغوان بر آب روان،

و

شناور

با نغمه و نوید، می آرد سوی ما!

ما بر کرانهٔ فرات

یواخیم سارتوریوس

ترجمهٔ رحیم غلامی

پذیرش، اقتباس و ترکیب استادانه و خلاقانه ادبیات خارجی، مؤلفه ای شاخص از هنر پویا و شناور دوران اخیر گوته میباشد. ناگفته پیداست که جهانی بودن در رگ و خون گوته آمیخته بود. او در آفاق و انفس سیر کرده و در مراودات خویش با دیگران در اوج فرهیختگی به تمام فضایل و کرامات آراسته بود.

اما، به دفعات و بسیار پیش می‌آید، که این هنرمند خلاق، همو که بیگانه را در زوایای وجود خویش پیدا کرده، با ذوق و هنر پویای خود ما را به روشهای بدیع بر سر شوق و طرب می آورد. درخشنده ترین شاهد این مدعا بی شک 'دیوان غربی-شرقی' گوته است. شعرِ 'آواز و آفریدن، ترانه و تنیدن، نغمه و نوید' در آغاز دیوان: یعنی در 'مُغَنّی نامه' می‌آید. سراینده بی تردید خود گوته است، و از مضامین اشعار کتاب او، رویکرد شاعر به دنیای خاور میباشد، همراه تمام مؤلفه هایی که حاکی از اشتیاق او به شرق است.

خیلی مجمل بگوییم، خاستگاه 'دیوان غربی-شرقی' ریشه در دو انگیزه دارد: ابتدا آشنایی گوته با شاعر فارسی زبان یعنی حافظ در سال ۱۸۱۴ از طریق ترجمه جوزف فون هامر در همان سال، و دیگری عشق پیری او برای ماریان فون ویلمِر، همسر جوان و با نشاط یک بانک دار، در تابستان ۱۸۱۵.

در شعر 'ترانه و تنیدن' میتوان آثار این دو نیروی درخشنده را یکجا در عبارت 'آتش جان من' مشاهده کرد، که او در وصف عشق ناکام و پنهانش برای این زن جوان میسراید، عشقی که او میبایست، در تسلیم و احترام به دربار [کذا] و همسرش کریستین

۱۷

فون گوته، از آن دست میکشید؛ و دیگری در عبارت 'عنصر سیّال' که استعاره ای است برای شعر شرق، شعری که در صورت و بیان آزاد و رها بوده و حد و مرز نمیشناسد. این شعر برخاسته از دردها و اشتیاق های ذهنی است، در حالی که هم آفریننده و مُبّین و هم 'آرام بخش' و 'سامان دهندهٔ' آن دردها و اشتیاق ها میباشد.

سرچشمهٔ 'دیوان' ریشه در اکتشافات و سیر و سلوک ادبی گوته در 'مهد مشرق زمین' دارد، و به گفتهٔ خود گوته، سیر ادبی او به 'موطن اصلی بشر' است. با وجود اینکه حافظ در کانون توجه و تأملات و تبلور تفکرات و اندیشه های شاعرانه گوته بود، او جمله آحاد فرهنگهای خاور میانه را نیز مطالعه کرد و از نزدیک با آنها مبادلات فرهنگی و ادبی داشت، و تمام سفرنامه های منتشر شده راجع به خاور میانه، ایران و آسیای میانه را خوانده بود. همچنین میدانیم که تلاشهای شایانی نمود تا خطّاطی این مرز و بوم را فراگیرد، و نام 'زلیخا' را به خط فارسی بر دم پایی هایی که به ماریان فون ویلِمِر هدیه داد گلدوزی کرده بود.

گوته ― همان گونه که ما نیز امروز بر آن واقف هستیم ― خوب میدانست اصل شعر ریشه در سواحل دجله و فرات داشته است. نویسندهٔ فرانسوی، موریس بلانشو، مینویسد که سومریان باستان نقش رؤیاهای خود را بر کلوخ میکشیدند و به داخل رود می انداختند. بلانشو ادعا میکند که تکه های کلوخ نمادی از کتاب و شعر بوده، و رود نشان مردم میباشد. گوته خویش را با این نمادهای قدیم باستانی هم نوا و یگانه میداند. او، با نام بردن از فرات، آشکارا به بین النهرین اشاره میکند. منظور او از 'ما' در شعرش شاعران مشرق زمین هستند که او خود را هم قطار آنان میبیند.

گوته در شعرش در مقابل شاعران مشرق زمین از 'یونانیان' نام میبرد؛ اما، بجای انتخاب پیکر تراشی یونانی از سنگهای مرمر به عنوان مثال خویش، از میان هنرهای تجسمی یونانیان باستان، که مثالی محتملتر مینمود، کار سرشتنِ گِل خام را به یونانیان نسبت میدهد، تا تناسب میان این کار و 'عنصر سیّال' را مراعات کند، مبادا ما از او شخصیتی 'ضد-کلاسیک' در خاطر آوریم. از همه اینها گذشته، گوته که خود را پیشتر پیرو یونانیان میبینند، بسیار تلاش دارد تا قرابت و تناسبی میان تندیس سازان یونان باستان و شاعران پارسی زبان قرون میانه برقرار سازد، و این بینشی است که او در 'دیوان' صریحاً اظهار میدارد، بینشی که در آن خاور و باختر و غرب و شرق به شکل جدایی ناپذیری به یکدیگر متصل هستند.

در آمدن و کشیده شدن یونانی در سماع در اثر کاری که خود او خلق کرده است، محتملا اشاره ای است به داستان پوگمالیون در شعر شاعر رومی، اووید، که عاشق مجسمه ای شد که خود او از عاج تراشیده بود، یا به اسطورهٔ پرومتئوس اشاره دارد که، از گِل، مجسمه مردم میساخت و سپس آتنا در آنها روح و زندگی میدمید. او این 'برانگیخته شدن' یا 'سماع' و از خود بیخود شدن را با آرامش و سرور شاعران مشرق زمین مقایسه میکنند که بر فرات سفر کرده و آتش درون خویش را با خواندن آوازی آرام میکنند.

ابیات پایانی این شعر توصیف کنندهٔ معجزه ای هستند که در آن آب در جنبش و گردشِ خود تبدیل به نغمه ای سیّال و ماندنی به نام آواز شده، و 'چون گوی معلّق بر سما' در دستان توانای شاعر ابدی میگردد. هِندریک بیروس به تمثیل مشابهی در متنی نوشتهٔ یاکوب گِریم اشاره کرده است. گِریم در پیشگفتار بر شعر 'هاینزریشِ فقیر'، نوشته

هارتمن فون آئو، مینویسد که 'خارج از حوزه ادبیات عامه، تنها بزرگترین شاعران اعصار هستند که دستان توانای‌شان قدرت و نبوغ گرد آوری آب 'چون گوی معلّق' را دارند، آبی که دیگران بایستی آن را در قالبهای مادی بریزند تا حمل کنند'.

هرچه در شعر هست در حرکت و جنبشی موزون و زیبا حول نقطهٔ بودن است، و مانند گویِ آبی در فضا شناور است! اما معجزه حقیقی اینجاست که چگونه شعری چنان ثقیل، با مضامین عظیم، چنین سهل و روان در بیان آمده و چون دُرّی گهربار میدرخشد.

"دار الأمل للتعقل والانسجام"

مقابلة مع دانيال بارنبويم

هل تعتقد حقاً أن أكاديمية بارنبويم-سعيد يمكن أن تسهم في التوصل إلى حل سلمي فيما يخص الصراع في الشرق الأوسط؟

بالتأكيد ولكن ليس على المدى القصير — على المدى الطويل كل شيء محتمل. عندما قمت أنا وإدوارد سعيد بتأسيس أوركسترا الديوان الغربي-الشرقي في عام ١٩٩٩، عندها ستون في المئة من الموسيقيين لم يكونوا قد شاركوا في أي أوركسترا من قبل، وأربعون في المئة منهم لم يحضر أي حفل أوركسترا مباشر قطّ. ولكن بعد ثمان سنوات، قمنا بتأدية مقطوعة "تنويعات لأوركسترا" الصعبة والمعقدة لأرنولد شونبرغ في سالزبورغ، وهو إنجاز لم يتوقع أحد من قبل أن نحققه. إنَّ تطوراً كهذا يمكن أن يحدث في الصراع السياسي في الشرق الأوسط أيضاً. إنها عملية لا تستثني — أو لا يجب أن تستثني — الأمل في السلام والمصالحة.

إلى أي مدى هناك انسجام حقيقي بين الموسيقيين في أوركسترا الديوان الغربي-الشرقي؟

بالطبع هناك اختلافات ونقاشات بين بعضهم البعض. وعند وجود اختلاف فإن ذلك يقود إلى الوصول الى تسوية وتقديم تنازلات مثلما هو الحال في أي نظام سياسي مستقل. فلقد استطاعوا التحرر من الكثير من الأيديولوجيات الفكرية لكثير من آبائهم وأمهاتهم وأصدقائهم وإن الوصول الى ذلك ممكن عند السماح بتفهم، وربما حتى قبول، قصة الطرف الآخر. وكدليل على هذا الانفتاح قيام إسرائيلي وسوري بأداء المقطع الموسيقي ذاته سوية، ثم تناول الطعام معاً وتجاذب أطراف الحديث، والتي هي بالتأكيد تجربة فريدة لكليهما

لأن قيام السوري الذي طالما اعتبر أن كل الإسرائيليين أعداء بالاستماع الى إسرائيلي وربما للمرة الأولى يمكن أن يساهم في استيعاب وتفهم الطرف الإسرائيلي. والشيء ذاته ينطبق على الشخص الإسرائيلي أيضاً. لذلك قد تكون الأوركسترا رمزاً حياً لمستقبل أفضل في الشرق الأوسط، والكثير من الموسيقيين يبادلونني نفس الشعور، ولهذا السبب فهم متلاحمون.

لماذا أسست أكاديميتك في ألمانيا بدلاً من أي مكان أخر في الشرق الأوسط؟

لسبب واحد، وهو أن برلين اليوم هي عاصمة الموسيقى في العالم. أضف إلى ذلك أن الوضع السياسي في الشرق الأوسط يجعل تحقيق مثل هذا المشروع مستحيل فعلياً وللأسف إن الأمور هناك خارج السيطرة ولكن ليس ميؤوساً منها. إن العديد من أصدقائنا يعتقدون أن الأكاديمية في برلين هي عبارة عن مشروع مثالي. وقد يكون هذا صحيحاً بعض الشيء ولكن ليس كل مثالي هو خطأ وغير قابل للتطبيق، وكمثال على ذلك إعادة توحيد شطري ألمانيا. لذلك فإنه بالإمكان اعتبار تأسيس الأكاديمية هي محاولة غير عادية وفريدة لدعم التقارب السياسي من خلال الموسيقى. وهدف هذا التقارب هو إيجاد تفاهم متبادل لأن الموسيقى هي لغة عالمية ولا توجد كلمة "عدو" بين مفرداتها. إن حكومة ألمانيا الاتحادية ومدينة برلين الراعيتان لهذا المشروع — واللتان أشكر دعمهما — لا تنظران إلى هذا المشروع بشكل متغاير. فعندما قمت بالعزف في مدينة رام الله للمرة الأولى أمام مائتي طفل فلسطيني، اقتربت مني فتاة فقمت بسؤالها: "هل أنت سعيدة أنني هنا؟" فكان جوابها الذي لن أنساه أبداً "نعم، أنا سعيدة جداً لأنك أول شيء يأتي من إسرائيل وليس بجندياً أو دبابة". في ذلك الوقت لم يكن لهذه الفتاة أن تتخيل يوماً ترى فيه اسرائيلياً بدون زي عسكري، أو أشياء إسرائيلية ليست بمركبة عسكرية. في الأكاديمية يمكن للشباب العربي والإسرائيلي التغلب على الأفكار السلبية عن العالم والتخلص منها، وعند عودتهم إلى أوطانهم، يأخذون

معهم ليس فقط تجربة صنع الموسيقى سوياً، ولكن أيضاً صداقات جديدة تتخطى الحدود. عندها ستكون الأكاديمية داراً للأمل في التعقل والانسجام.

هل من الممكن أنك تنسب إلى الموسيقى قوة أكثر مما لها في الحقيقة؟

إن أي سمفونية أو رباعية أو أوبرا لن تقوم بتغيير العالم كلياً، ولكن يمكن للموسيقى أن تقوم بالتأثير على كل واحد منا. وبالطبع فإن الموسيقى ذات تأثير قوي لأن لها وجود مادي، ولأنها تعبير مجسد لروح الإنسان، يتجاوز عالم الأفكار الصرفة. إنها تجمع كل جانب من جوانب الوجود الإنساني وإن إيقاعها يغذي الدماغ والقلب والحالات المزاجية. وكل واحد منا يتفاعل مع الموسيقى في كل جانب من هذه الجوانب مما يجعل الموسيقى قوية جداً. فالموسيقى أقوى من الكلمات وحتى في المقطوعات الحزينة ستجد أن هنالك بارقة من الأمل في جوانبها. وبسبب ذلك فإن الموسيقى توحد الوجود الإنساني معاً، وفي الوقت الحاضر يمكن سماع الموسيقى على كوكبنا أكثر من أي وقت مضى في تاريخها، فهي تمثل أجمل صيغ العولمة.

هل تعتقد أن ألمانيا يمكن أن تقوم بدور خاص، أو أنه ينبغي لها أن تلعب دورا خاصا عن طريق مساهماتها بأكاديمية بارنبويم-سعيد؟

قمت منذ طفولتي بالسفر الى جميع أنحاء العالم وكان هذا جزء من حياتي ومسيرتي في تأليف الموسيقى. لذلك فأنا أعتبر نفسي مواطناً من إسرائيل وإسبانيا والأرجنتين وفلسطين. ولكن لا أعلم بوجود بلد آخر قام بما قامت به ألمانيا عند الحديث عن التاريخ والشعور بالذنب من ماضيها على الأخص فيما يتعلق بالمحرقة. ولذلك فإن الحفاظ على حسن العلاقات السياسية والثقافية مع إسرائيل هو جزء من العقيدة التي تأسست عليها الدولة الألمانية — كما أكد جميع مستشاري ألمانيا، والمستشارة ميركل على وجه التحديد. ولهذا

فإن لألمانيا رغبة قوية في الاعتدال وإيجاد حل سلمي للصراع في الشرق الأوسط أكثر من أي بلد أخر، ولكن بدون وجود تعاون من جميع الجهات فإن الحل سيكون مستحيلاً. أحياناً أتخيل انعقاد مؤتمر في الشرق الأوسط يمكن أن يساهم حقاً في تحقيق السلام في المنطقة، تماماً مثل سيمفونية تعزف من قبل الخريجين من أكاديميتنا في برلين — أنه حلم بالتأكيد ...

ما المعزوفة التي ستقوم بتأديتها؟

ربما المقطوعة التاسعة لبيتهوفن: "هو الذي يعرف الفخر والسرور من صداقة ثابتة وقوية". وطالما أننا نتحدث عن الدور الألماني الخاص في هذا المجال ينبغي أن نذكر أنها المركز الرئيسي في عالم الموسيقى. فهناك أكثر من ثمانين داراً للأوبرا، وأكثر من مائة وثلاثون فرقة موسيقية من الدرجة الأولى أي ما يعادل ثلث فرق الأوركسترا السيمفونية المهنية في جميع أنحاء العالم. لذلك فإنه يوجد هنا إرث نابض بالحياة من الكلاسيكية الألمانية والنمساوية والعصر الرومانسي والموسيقى الحديثة، ومع كل مقطوعة تعزف لباخ أو بيتهوفن في أي مكان في العالم تنتشر أفكار ثقافة ألمانية أكثر جمالا واستدامة من أي صادرات سلاح. وما الأوركسترات السيمفونية الكبيرة إلا دليل على دور ألمانيا في هذا المجال، وذلك بالإضافة إلى ما يقارب ٧٥٠ خريجاً سنوياً من أكاديميات ألمانيا الموسيقية على الرغم من أن العديد منهم لا يبقى في ألمانيا. يحمل الخريجون العرب والإسرائيليين من الأكاديمية رسالة جديدة عند عودتهم الى أوطانهم وهي أن الاحترام المتبادل ليس فقط ممكناً بل إنه ضروري إذا أراد الناس العمل والعيش جنباً إلى جنب في وئام وانسجام وحينئذ سينبغي على الناس الاستماع إليهم.

أجرى المقابلة وولفغانغ بينكين